Eduard Maco Hudson

The second War of Independence in America

Eduard Maco Hudson

The second War of Independence in America

ISBN/EAN: 9783337115913

Printed in Europe, USA, Canada, Australia, Japan

Cover: Foto ©ninafisch / pixelio.de

More available books at **www.hansebooks.com**

THE

SECOND WAR OF INDEPENDENCE

IN AMERICA

BY

E. M. HUDSON

JURIS UTRIUSQUE DOCTOR, FELLOW OF THE GEOGRAPHICAL SOCIETY OF BERLIN,
LATE ACTING SECRETARY OF LEGATION TO THE AMERICAN
MISSION TO THE COURT OF PRUSSIA.

TRANSLATED BY THE AUTHOR

FROM THE SECOND REVISED AND ENLARGED GERMAN EDITION

WITH AN INTRODUCTION BY BOLLING A. POPE

LONDON

LONGMAN, GREEN, LONGMAN, ROBERTS, & GREEN

1863

PREFACE

TO

THE SECOND GERMAN EDITION.

THE motive for the publication of ' The Second War
of Independence in America,' which appeared in
January last, was the earnest desire, by means of a
short and conscientious exposition of the American
question, to correct, as far as possible, the erroneous
notions which had been propagated in Germany with
regard to this unholy conflict. The attention with
which every event in the course of this war is followed, proves how intimately the sympathies and
interests of Europe are concerned in it.

Since the appearance of the first edition some
changes have taken place in the condition of things.
Wherever these have been of any importance, I have
communicated them in notes or additions, and have
called attention to their significance. In general, it

may be remarked that the conduct of the war on the part of the Confederates has been changed. Without seeking now, as formerly, to check the enemy on the frontiers of the Southern territory, it appears to be the intention of the Southern Government to draw him into the heart of the South; for there the South will be able to oppose him, deprived of the protection of his navy, with equal arms and with greater prospect of success.

The lack of authentic information at that time was a sufficient ground for the publication of this volume. In consequence of the total suspension of postal communication between the South and Europe, no accounts of transpiring events were able to reach us; and thus the people of Europe were able to base their judgement only upon statements both one-sided and coloured to suit party-purpose. The present condition of the press in the Northern States, however, is a still greater inducement for a caution against the credibility of all news emanating from that source. From the beginning, the South has suffered severely from the difficulty of postal communication with Europe, as the North has by this means been enabled to deceive the nations of Europe. At the present moment, the state of affairs is far more aggravated. The Northern Government have issued a proclamation,

prohibiting the publication of a word with reference
to the events of the war, without special permission.
And when it is borne in mind that the Federal
Government are pledged to crush the rebellion by
May 1, in order to avert European intervention, it
will appear evident that no news favourable to the
South can be expected from the North. We shall,
however, now be able to estimate the value to be
attached to Northern accounts.

On many sides regret has been expressed through
the press that no special examination had been made
of the question of Slavery in the former edition. I
have, therefore, determined to add, as a supplement,
a particular chapter on the condition of the slaves in
America. This chapter is limited, however, to the
actual condition of the African slaves, with brief
reference to the question of emancipation. The moral
side of Slavery I have left undiscussed.

No one who examines well all the circumstances
can, in the face of these brief intimations, fail to be
convinced that the North, in inscribing emancipation
of the slaves upon its banner as the cause of the war
against the South, has acted with an entire disregard of truth; and this, in order to win the approval
of the European States for its war of conquest, and
to frustrate the recognition of the Southern States

as an independent power, or at least to delay it as
long as possible, for the sake of self-preservation.
An impartial examination of the action of the North
towards its own emancipated slaves, which have not
been made equals of the whites, and the endeavour,
which it has never attempted to conceal, to disembarrass
itself of the emancipated negroes, favoured with only
inferior rights, by sending them beyond its borders,
will prove to the conviction of any one that it is out
of no considerations of humanity that the North is
induced to raise such a 'hue and cry' about Slavery
in the South.   On the other hand, it will be evident
to those whose attention is directed to the peculiarities of the country and the character of the
negro, that an emancipation of the slaves, in their
own interest as well as in that of the country, could
not, with any degree of reason, be effected by a
sudden and hasty act; but that in all cases, supposing emancipation to be desirable, well-matured
plans of transition would be necessary to elevate the
negro-race, so far below the whites in the scale of
developement, to a condition for enjoying liberty,
without certain destruction to itself and to the
country.   The Abolitionists would, without any
sacrifice on their part, consecrate the country and
its inhabitants to destruction for the sake of an idea,

and would apply to a condition, which they characterise as a malady, a radical cure which they refused to apply to their own body, as long as it was suffering from a similar one.

The want of accurate and true representations of the causes and objects of the war, because all accounts emanated from the North, has influenced the press of Germany warmly to espouse the cause of the Federal Government. It is, nevertheless, undeniable that the press has recently been more enlightened; but still prejudices, once awakened, have remained, as it was the impression in Europe that the abolition of Slavery was the great humanitarian object of the war in America. In confirmation of my own views upon the American question, I refer to the letter of Captain M. F. Maury to Admiral Fitzroy. The writer, who is well known throughout Europe for his extensive scientific attainments, gives a clear statement of the origin of the difficulty, criticises the measures of Lincoln, and exposes the resources of the South and the reasons for its eventual success.

With a quiet conscience, therefore, may I leave the final decision about this war to the intelligent public, who know very well that the faults of State Government cannot be corrected by *brilliant theories.*

I may now lay aside my pen with the consciousness, equally free from over-estimation and self-praise, that I have fearlessly followed the voice of truth in contributing my mite, as in duty bound, to the welfare of my native land.

BERLIN: *March* 28, 1862.

CONTENTS.

CHAPTER IV.

CHAPTER V.

CHAPTER VI.

INTRODUCTION.

The interest evinced by the British public for every-thing pertaining to the war in America, and the success which the 'Second War of Independence in America' has obtained in scientific and political circles in Germany, have induced Mr. Hudson to reproduce it in England. The second German edition has been made the basis of the English, some points being treated more in detail, while others, perhaps too elementary for this stage of the American war, have been omitted.

The constitutional right of secession is developed at length, and no point of discussion has been omitted; while the author has given special pro-minence to the historical foundation of the right.

The causes which led to the exercise of this right will be found all duly arrayed, and prominent among them the original antipathy and antagonism of the Northern and Southern colonists, and the influences which have tended to keep these alive and active. Indeed, when we seek to determine the true character

of these two nations by the experience of the present
war, we are astonished that they could have lived so
long under the same government. This difference
was one of the principal reasons for the ardent attachment of the Southern people to the doctrine of
' State Rights.' All the elements of distinct national
life being present, the South, plastic from the heat of
political passion and war, has been moulded by her
leaders into a nation as complete in all that is essential to the name, as though she were as old as the
' Celestial Empire.'

The subject of Slavery is briefly but fully treated.
Here the author has avoided no question but that of
the abstract right or wrong involved, deeming, very
properly, this to be a point the discussion of which
not being practical would be barren of results. He
takes a great fact, and treats it in its practical bearings, leaving to time the solution of those problems
which can never be determined by theoretical discussions, by fanatical abuse and interference, or
by treaties which could never have any practical
effect if made. This portion of the work embraces
an historical sketch of African Slavery in the United
States, and an exposition of the legal condition of the
negro (free and slave) in America, thereby utterly
confounding those calumniators of the South who
have proclaimed the slave to be in the Southern code
only a ' chattel.' Unfortunately, the European public

seem to have been led, certainly not by the autho-
rized organs of the Confederate States, to believe that
the South was prepared to allow the condition of her
negro population to be determined by the European
powers. Nothing could be further from her intentions, since the question does not fall within the
jurisdiction of the powers delegated to the Confederate Government. Moreover, it would be an
endorsement of all the calumnies of her enemies, the
admission that Europe knows her internal condition
and interests better than herself, and is actuated by
higher motives of humanity; and finally, it would be
a relinquishment of the dearest right of sovereignty,
impossible to a proud and sensitive people.

The unparalleled growth of the United States in
wealth, population, and power has been viewed with
varied feelings by the different countries and classes
of Europe. According to the peculiar interests or
policy of the governments and people, or the political
theories which happened to prevail with a given
class, have opinions been formed. Upon the whole,
the Union carried with it the moral weight of success, except with a few far-seeing thinkers. This
mighty empire fell hopelessly at a time, when even
men hostile to its political ideas were upon the point
of acknowledging its success. The great majority
in the South had long seen the approach of the cata-
strophe, and were divided only as to the best time and

means for securing themselves from a government that was fast becoming a tyranny of the most oppressive character. At the time of the secession of the Southern States, there was a party, largely in the minority, which thought that the appropriate time for separation had not arrived, and that in case of war the South, being unprepared, would be at a great disadvantage. In this party was to be found what of sentiment for the common history still existed, together with those interests which in case of a war are always the first to suffer. The right of secession was doubted by no party in the South; it was with all purely a question of time and expediency. The secession of the South took the North by surprise, which, not at first appreciating that it was more than the impulse of sudden passion, affected to consider it as something exceedingly farcical, of which the South would soon become most heartily ashamed. How much of this was affected, and how much was the result of ignorance or policy, it is impossible to determine. Yet as the idea gained ground that the movement had a real meaning and a purpose, the Abolitionists who had expressed their joy to be rid of the South, the more moderate Republicans who had disavowed any desire to preserve the Union by force, and the Democrats, who had till then been friendly to the South, seeing that great political and material interests were at stake, united to form that mass of fanaticism, hate, hypocrisy, and vandalism which has disgraced the nineteenth century. When the news of the dissolution of the Union reached Europe, there was, in England at least, a feeling of relief; for every trace of conservatism had disappeared from the Government; while the foreign policy had come to be determined by the foreign population and the party of 'Manifest Destiny' at the hustings. Under the influence of the lawless and socialistic elements from Europe, and the extreme democratic ideas prevalent in the North, the right of suffrage had lost its dignity, and political power had passed into the hands of those least capable of using it well. There was one party in Europe that saw the dissolution with deep and unconcealed disappointment. With the fall of the Union were lost to the party of revolution its hopes of powerful aid from that quarter, for re- moving the remaining restrictions upon their theory of universal equality. They had always hated the South, but now their hatred knew no bounds; and, with the Republican party of the North, they de- manded a war of extermination. A misconception as to the true character of the Union produced at first coolness on the part of the Conservatives, the natural allies of the South, which has happily passed away with the error that caused it. The whole of Europe, misled by the malignant misrepresentations of the Abolitionists of Europe and America, saw little

occasion for sympathy in the picture of a nation composed of a few cruel and voluptuous slaveholders, a
large mass of 'white trash,' and millions of Africans
smarting from the lash and groaning under the bur-
dens of their taskmasters.   Those interested in those
branches of commerce and manufactures which were
affected by the hostilities, naturally looked upon the
South as a disturber of the public peace, asking few
questions about the right or wrong of her actions.
If, at the commencement of the war, the South had
a friend in Europe, there was no evidence of the fact.
Some may have wished her success for political
reasons, but there was no sentiment of sympathy for
her cause, and but little hope that she would succeed
in the unequal contest, while her enemies were
confident of her speedy subjugation.

But what are the results of a war of nearly two
years ? Considering the populations engaged, and
the attending circumstances, they characterise it as
a war almost unparalleled in history. All the pre-
dictions of the enemies of the South have been
falsified ; while her bold and defiant confidence,
thought to be the result of ignorance, has been more
than justified by the almost romantic success of her
arms. We have seen a government spring into
existence, exercising with dignity and consummate
skill almost unlimited powers, without impairing the
liberty of the individual.   We have seen a people in

the want of all the appliances of war, and supposed to be enervated by indolence and vice, accomplish all that could have been expected from a nation with a highly developed industrial and military organization. We have seen an army badly armed and equipped supply itself from its rich, numerous, and boasting enemy. We have seen a nation act as an unit, and find its strength where friends and foes had sought its weakness. In fine, every evidence of unity, vitality, courage, perseverance, and success has been presented to the world; and, upon the whole, the South has gained moral as well as physical victories, and has won the sympathy of all who admire heroic spirit, and abhor treachery, corruption, imbecility, and cruelty. In the meantime, she has invited the most searching scrutiny of her internal condition and institutions, knowing, as she does, that ignorance of·these has been the greatest obstacle in her way. It is highly probable that, had the governments of Europe had a clear view of the true state of America at the commencement of the struggle, their policy would have been somewhat different.

Apart from the causes which led to the dissolution, it was best for the world and for America itself that disunion should have taken place; for the idea of future irresistible power, and the absence of all conservative restraints, would soon have rendered peace impossible; and had the warlike enthusiasm of xx

the combined nation once engaged it in war with a
foreign power, it would have been the bloodiest of
history. For America it was best, since the political
system was fast demoralizing the people; and the
only hope was in the formation of two governments,
by which a balance of power might be created on
that continent, and with it more conservative
political tendencies. Besides, the territory of the
Union was too large to be longer well-governed;
and this of itself would have made dissolution inevitable. War has its evils; but, upon the whole, a
long peace has evils perhaps equally great, which can
only be remedied by war. In addition to the ill
effects of a too-long peace, America had peculiar
necessity for internal war, in order that the political
and material forces of the continent should be mea-
sured, both for the benefit of herself and of Europe,
as upon this point the ignorance seemed to be almost
universal. Viewed in this light, it appears, then, that
disunion was inevitable and desirable; and that war
was necessary as a solid foundation for a long peace,
undisturbed by those quarrels which take place
between neighbours unacquainted with the horrors
of a war brought home to themselves, and ignorant
of their mutual strength. Great Britain, for obvious
reasons, felt the deepest interest in what transpired
in America. It was the fall of her great future rival,
the peculiarities of whose diplomacy she had learned

to appreciate, and whose cotton-fields would have been so potent for evil in the event.of war. She saw that America, under the political guidance of the North, would inaugurate that system under which her own industrial grandeur had been built up, and which she has so recently learned to be a ruinous error. Trembling for her commercial sceptre, her relief must have been more profound than has ever been acknowledged. The question of the blockade came up and lessened somewhat this sense of satisfaction, in itself perfectly justifiable. But Manchester had studied political economy, which teaches that ' supply is regulated by demand.' And there were India, and Egypt, and Turkey, and Brazil, and Australia, and the West Indies, and Central America, and Mexico, and Africa, all ready to take part in this great plan for emancipating British industry from the American ' monopoly.' Besides, a blockade of the Southern ports, it was seen, would relieve the market of the excess of cotton cloths, and though a slight violation of Manchester philosophy, if not continued too long, might act beneficially as a stimulant for opening new cotton-fields. It has long been the dream of England to become totally independent of foreign countries for the supply of raw material for her manufactures, and it had always been especially galling to see herself dependent on the United States for her chief supply of cotton. This feeling had extended to the system of labour itself which produced it, and explains, much more than the English themselves are perhaps aware, their *special* hatred to negro slavery in the South. The South had also imprudently expressed the hope that the necessity for cotton would force England to prevent the blockade of her ports; and it was easy to see, by consulting the expressions of the various organs of public opinion at the time, that the English people felt it to be almost a national insult to suppose that they would be influenced in their political course by interest. It is difficult to conceive that England has been influenced as much by the threats of the Government at Washington as the world has been led to believe.

The idea that England, hating the institutions of each section, calmly awaits the ruin of both, is inconsistent with her character for humanity, and a clear view of her own interests. Though a rival, they have furnished her with the best market in which to buy and sell, and it is impossible to see how their ruin could result in her benefit.

The opinion of those who maintain that action of any kind whatever on the part of Europe, with regard to America, would only tend to lengthen the war and increase its bitterness, are not justified by experience or history, and are contrary to public opinion in America.

The commercial interests have been quieted by the repeated intimation of the danger of a war, a danger existing only in the imagination of the timid, or of those totally unacquainted with the Yankee character. Those engaged in manufactures have been told that no action short of war would relieve their sufferings, while their fears about the destruction of their interests were quieted by the hope that the misfortune would be of short duration.

The Radicals did not desire the termination of the war, their motto being sympathy and alliance with the North.

The war in America means not only the loss of that great political power so necessary to the North for her commercial and industrial schemes, but it means the loss of the very foundation of her naval and industrial greatness. The loss of the West will soon follow that of the South, already accomplished. It is useless for England to seek to make a friend of this people without a nationality; it is impossible. Their interests are diametrically opposed to hers, and of this the Morrill Tariff is a sufficient confirmation. Politically, she will gravitate anywhere else than towards England.

Observed from the point of their geographical relations, climate, productions, stage of industrial developement, origin, character, and political interests, one cannot fail to be struck with the community of

interests between Great Britain and the Confederate
States.   The one a great manufacturer and importer
of raw materials, the other a great producer of raw
materials and importer of manufactured articles; the
one possessing a great commercial navy, the other
producing in quantities, whose increase is hardly to
be limited, all those products most adapted to the
support of a large commercial navy; the one rich
and mature, the other young, but full of ardour and
enterprise, descended from England, speaking her
language, possessing the same laws, and, for the most
part, holding the same political ideas.   The importance of the countries on the Mississippi and around
the Gulf of Mexico to England, needs no explana-
tion; but, to make them fully available for her purposes, it is absolutely necessary that a powerful and
well-ordered government should exist in the Southern
States, the policy of which should be dictated by
their obvious interests, and not by those of New
England.   Certain social accidents, conflicting with
opinions that have gained ground only within the
last sixty years, are thought by some to be sufficient
to vitiate the benefit of this mutual interest. Nothing
could be more false, and a more intimate mutual
acquaintance would prove its falsity.   Those who
believe that it is the duty of England to demand
conditions from the South in her present difficulties,
may be referred to the result of the contest between

Boreas and the Sun, of which a lonely traveller was
the object.   Free Trade is obviously to the interest
of the Confederate States, yet there is reason to fear
that, should the war continue, the Government of
the Confederate States will encounter great difficulties
in carrying out this policy, since the blockade has compelled the South to manufacture for herself.   Large
amounts of capital have been forced into this channel,
and when the war ceases this must, without protection, become a total loss.   It may well be asked,
whether it would be just to sacrifice those who have
saved the South, for the interest of those who saw
the blockade—the true cause of the great length of
the war—go into force without a protest.   The wedge
once introduced, we should in all probability have
the history of the protective system of the old Union,
which sprang up in this way, reenacted.   The large
national debt would also operate in the same direction, and have a stronger ground for its defence in
the fact that it would lighten in a high degree direct
taxation.

The most important industrial considerations
arising from the war, and consequent blockade, are
the effects upon the cotton interests of Great Britain
and the Confederate States.   Allusion to this subject
must naturally be very incomplete here, as a careful
investigation of all the questions involved would
demand a separate volume.

A little over a century ago commenced in England that series of inventions which render it the most important era in her commercial history. Coincident with the improvements in the machinery for spinning cotton and weaving cotton cloth, came into operation the improvements in the application of steam power. Immediately after the above-mentioned inventions for the manufacture of cotton, followed that of the cotton gin, for separating the wool from the seed, an invention destined to revolutionise commerce. This gave the first impetus to the culture of cotton in the South, the rapid development of which furnishes the most remarkable facts in the history of industry. Before the commencement of the cotton trade between Europe and the present Confederate States, the manufacture of cotton had slowly but steadily increased in England. The importation of cotton wool amounted in 1795 to 22,600,000 lbs., of which only 100,000 lbs. came from the East Indies. The cotton gin was introduced in 1793, and in 1794 1,601,760 lbs. and in 1795 5,276,300 lbs. of cotton were exported from the South. The total quantity of cotton exported from the South to Europe in 1860 was 1,767,686,338 lbs., valued at 191,806,555 dollars. This estimate of value does not of course include that of 1,000,000 of bales retained and consumed mostly in New England. This gives an additional

500,000,000 lbs. to the cotton production of the
South, which may be valued at 50,000,000 dollars.
The amount of capital invested in the manufacture
of cotton in Great Britain in 1787 was 1,000,000*l*.,
the number of operatives employed being about
60,000. The total import of cotton into Great
Britain in 1860 was 1,390,938,752 lbs., of which
1,115,890,608 lbs. were imported from the United
States; 204,141,168 lbs. from the East Indies;
1,050,784 lbs. from the West Indies; 17,286,864 lbs.
from the Brazils; and 52,369,328 lbs. from all
other countries. Of the whole amount imported,
1,140,510,112 lbs. were retained for British manufactures. The declared value of cotton yarns and
goods exported in 1860 was 44,104,636*l*., being about
4,100,000*l*. less than in 1859. The cheapness of
cotton goods, as well as the enormous increase in
the wealth of the country produced by the cotton
trade, has been a source of incalculable benefit to
all classes, and to all branches of industry. This
cheapness of one of the principal necessaries of
life has raised the standard of comfort and caused
a greater demand for luxuries, affording increased
means for their gratification. This fact applies
not only to Great Britain, but to all other countries
where cotton cloths are largely consumed; so that
cotton may be considered one of the greatest agents
for increasing commerce and extending civilization.

It is an undisputed fact, that the steady and rapid increase of the production of cotton in the South, its convenience to the British manufacturer, and its cheapness and superior quality, have been the causes of the great increase in this branch of British industry.

There being no way of accounting for the position of America in the cotton trade, except by the operation of natural laws, it is of great importance to have these clearly in view in discussing the general question of the cotton supply, the results of the American war, and the possible effects of the blockade of the Southern ports upon the future of the cotton trade.

The cotton plant is not an indigenous growth of the Southern States, having been imported from the West Indies in 1621. It was first cultivated upon the Southern coast, but its culture has gradually been extended northward, until it forms the principal article of export from eight of the Southern States; and, great as is its production, there is every reason to believe that, without a revolution in the industry of the Southern States, it may be almost indefinitely increased.* In the extension of its cultivation northwards, the plant had to become acclimated; but such was the natural adaptation of the soil and climate to the growth of those kinds of cotton demanded by commerce, that the quality of the cotton has been

* Consult Introduction to *The South Vindicated.* Williams.

greatly improved. The exact part played by pecu-
liarity of soil is difficult to be determined, yet it
is well known that soils otherwise equally good are
not equally adapted to the production of cotton.
The influence of soil has nothing surprising in it,
since it has long been observed in the case of tobacco,
wine, coffee, and tea; it is, however, difficult to
separate this influence from that of climate, but there
is no doubt that it exists, and, in all probability, has
something to do with the superiority of American
cottons. The most important advantage which
America possesses is its climate, combining, as it
does, the characteristics of the tropical and of the
temperate zones. During the season for the growth
and maturition of the plant, the warm, moist winds
from the Gulf of Mexico equalize the temperature,
and occasion, as a rule, an abundant but not excessive fall of rain, so necessary to its successful
cultivation. To those well acquainted with the conditions necessary to the successful culture of cotton
it will be obvious, that a climate subject to long
droughts, alternating with a superabundance of
rain, are entirely unsuited to its culture, as, under
these circumstances, almost all the pods will be
'shed,' or stunted in their growth. During the
'picking' season the quantity of rain should be extremely small, and the weather clear and cool, which
is true of the climate of the South for the greater

part of the picking season. The winters, influenced
by northerly winds, are often quite cold for short
periods, even as far south as Florida, the fall of rain
being, as a rule, quite moderate. These two circumstances are very favourable to the fruitfulness of the
soil, and the first must diminish, to a considerable
extent, the injury to the cotton plant from insects
during its growth. This is a fact by no means to
be underrated, for it is a source of great annual loss,
amounting sometimes to the half, and, in exceptional
cases, to almost the whole of the crop. Fortunately,
the loss in America from this source, though always
considerable, is not uniform over the whole cotton
region, or even over the same plantation, so that the
uniformity in the production is not seriously disturbed. There are two disadvantages for the culti-.
vation of cotton in the Southern States, growing out
of the character of the winter season. Unlike most
of the cotton-producing countries of the world, the
winter is so cold that the seed must be sown annually; besides, the cotton plant is usually killed over
almost the whole of the cotton region by the middle
or last of October. Could the death of the plant be
delayed a month, it would be utterly impossible, with
the present supply of labour, to gather the crops
which the area at present cultivated would produce.
It is probable, however, that this would bring with
it a corresponding impoverishment of the soil. Not-

withstanding the comparative shortness of the season, the average yield per acre of clean cotton is much higher than in India. The yield per acre varies very much, even in the same locality, being for the whole South from 200 to 1,000 lbs.; while in India it is from 60 to 80 lbs. This fact of itself would be sufficient to cause us to doubt the capacity of India to compete successfully with America in the cotton market. It is true, that the cotton region of the South is in the summer season not free from climatic disadvantages, in certain portions intermittent fever prevailing, while in others yellow fever and cholera make their appearance at times. The negro is, however, comparatively little injured by the intermittent and seldom attacked by the yellow fever, and it may for this and other reasons be considered the natural climate of the negro. As regards healthfulness, it will compare favourably with any cotton-producing region of the world, which the statistics of population conclusively prove. The sparseness of population of the Southern States, and the fact that it is almost exclusively agricultural, which furnishes one of the most important conditions for enabling a nation to devote itself to a great export trade in grain, or raw material, are again reasons which increase its chances of success in a competition with India. One of the most potent causes of the success of the Southern States in the cultivation of cotton is to be found in the organization of their labour, and its relation to capital. This relation of labour and capital places both under the immediate direction of the most intelligent class, and renders their operations harmonious and certain, and, in effect, obtains the greatest results with the least loss of material and effort. The Southern States have built up a great railroad system which has cost about 250,000,000 dollars, and this almost exclusively by means of private home capital. This has perfected her system of internal intercourse, and brought the whole of her vast territory into rapid communication with the sea. Their geographical position with relation to Europe is again of great advantage, enabling them to deliver the raw material cheaper; for, when it is a question of the transport of an article so bulky in proportion to value, distance from market must always be a matter of prime consideration. When all these advantages are combined in one country in the hands of an energetic, intelligent, and skillful people, can there be any doubt of their superiority above other competitors? These advantages, together with the vast fields suited to the cultivation of cotton not yet brought into cultivation, considered with reference to the fact of the rapid increase of the labouring class of the Southern States, enable us to predict with certainty that, should no disturbance of the existing order of things take place, they will be more than able to meet the increased demand of the world. This is rendered more certain by the fact that the Southern States, in the greater portion of their territory, are not adapted to the cultivation of those tropical productions most likely to draw off the capital of the other cotton-growing regions from the cultivation of cotton. The planter of the Southern States appreciates his advantages to the fullest extent, and has no fear of foreign competition; in fact, he feels that to a certain extent the great demand for cotton has been a disadvantage to the South, for it has tended to cause the investment of too much capital in this direction.

The country next in importance as a competitor for supplying Europe with cotton is India. That this is the country upon which Europe must chiefly depend, as long as the supply from America is cut off by the blockade, is a fact almost universally admitted. At the time of the institution of the blockade, India stood second on the list of exporters of cotton to Europe. In 1795, the import of cotton from the East Indies into England amounted only to 100,000 lbs., while in 1860 it amounted to 204,141,608 lbs. Ages ago, India was a centre of the cultivation and manufacture of cotton; and at the time of the commencement of its culture in the Southern States, she was an exporter of cotton goods. At present, she imports from

England cotton yarns and goods, manufactured mostly from American cotton, to the amount of six or eight millions of pounds sterling. The same stimulus which was brought to bear upon other countries was extended to her, and yet we see how small has been her contribution to the cotton trade. It must be that great natural disadvantages exist, that the population do not possess the skill and capital necessary, or that they find the cultivation of grain, sugar, and indigo more profitable. All writers about India agree that if she is to be depended upon for supplying Europe with cotton, a much higher price must be paid than heretofore. Another fact, upon which all the world is agreed, is that up to this time the cotton supplied by India has been of a very inferior quality, and, for manufacturing purposes, must be mixed with the American cottons of bad colour, in the proportion of 15 to 85, the Indian cottons having all a fine colour. At present, one pound of Indian cotton yields but twelve ounces of yarn, while the same quantity of American cotton yields thirteen ounces and a half. Spinners obtain threepence halfpenny for converting one pound of Surat cotton into yarn, while they only obtain threepence farthing for converting the same quantity of American. It has been seen that the cotton of India is mixed with the inferior American sorts, in order to improve their colour, which would in a great degree account for the increased use of the former, and thus place it in the position of a commercial parasite. This importation of Indian cotton may also be taken as partially representing the amount of cotton freed by the displacement of the Indian manufactures, and not as an absolute increase of its production. There is nothing, however, which proves so conclusively the want of adaptation of East Indian cotton to the British market as the tables of cotton consumption; showing that, of the 524,000 bales imported, only 176,000 or 56,760,000 lbs. were retained for home consumption, the rest being taken by the Continent.

On account of the want of facts, it is impossible to speak of the suitedness of the soil of India to the cultivation of cotton. The fact that it requires from five to six acres of land for the production of a bale of 385 lbs. is conclusive as regards the question of productiveness; but as so many elements enter into this consideration, we must content ourselves with the discussion of those which are certain. The climate of India is purely tropical, and in this fact there is all the difference between success and failure. Of course, this does not apply equally to the whole of India; still it is true for that part upon which we must depend for some years to come. Mr. Laing, speaking of the dependence to be placed upon India for the future supply of cotton, says: ' India has one disadvantage only, the climate, and that is extreme.'

As singular as it may appear, the cotton seed of the
Southern States is exported to India; seeming to
show that there is an essential defect in the climate,
otherwise the Indian cotton must have improved
more than it has after ages of culture. Like the
potato, the cotton plant seems not perfect itself in it
native climate. The purely tropical character of the
climate of India, with its storms, long droughts, and
wet season, so disadvantageous to the cotton-plant, is
still favourable to the successful cultivation of indigo,
tea, coffee, and sugar. Even the extreme southern
portions of some of the Southern Gulf States is, by
reason of the more tropical character of the climate,
unfavourable to the growth of cotton; the plant
growing luxuriantly, but the wool becoming fine and
weak. There may be provinces in India which, by
reason of their possessing a more favourable climate,
were they developed and brought into communication with the sea, would be able to furnish a better
quality of cotton than has yet been sent to Europe.
The province of Dharwar seems to give some promise,
yet the success claimed, if certain, has been on a
small scale, and is not available for saving Lancashire
from ruin. We have seen that the Southern cotton
States are as yet sparsely settled, and almost purely
devoted to agriculture, the principal product being
cotton; for, as a rule, provisions are only raised in
sufficient quantities for home use. We know, more-

over, that should bread fall short, the granaries of
the Border States and of the North-West are at
their doors, to supply their wants much more cheaply
than India could supply hers in case of a similar
need.   India, with her 200,000,000 of souls, is ever
liable to famine, and cannot supply herself rapidly in
case of want, and then only at famine prices. We could
easily conceive of such a state of population that the
surplus of land to be employed in the raising of
articles not for food would be very limited.   This, it
is true, is not the case with India; yet the size of the
population, when considered in relation to the productiveness of her agriculture, is such, that provisions
must be dear, and thus any crop not cultivated for
food must be very profitable.   Now, upon a comparison of the profits of capital engaged in the
cultivation of grain with those engaged in the cultivation of cotton in India, we find that the advantage is largely in favour of grain; being by some
estimated even as high as 50 per cent. for ordinary
times.   This would, however, not' prevent the
increase of the cultivation of cotton, were it not that
other articles, as mentioned above, came first in order
with regard to the profitableness of their culture.
Mr. Laing estimates the increase of the area cultivated
in cotton necessary to meet the wants of Great
Britain at from ten to twenty million acres, which
to the initiated means years engaged in improving

land, and in changing the direction of capital.
Writers upon the cotton supply never tire in their
descriptions of the miserable condition of the Ryot,
his want of energy and enterprise, his Asiatic stub-
bornness in adhering to old customs and usages,
his partial dependence upon the capitalist, without
the advantages to himself and production growing
out of a more complete dependence. We are told of
his want of skill and honesty, in fact, of his total
degradation, and yet Mr. Laing informs us that it
is upon this class that Lancashire must depend in
case the American supply should be long withheld;
for he affirms that the European planters find it
more profitable to raise tea, and other articles of a
similar kind. According to this, the cultivation of
cotton by the Ryot is to a certain extent a thing of
habit, want of skill and capital for the cultivation of
other products, the developement of which would
rather tend to diminish the cultivation of cotton in
the districts best adapted to the culture of coffee,
tea, indigo, and sugar. The village capitalist has
been pictured as a tyrant ruling without mercy the
Ryot, and cheating the cotton consumer at will.
The merchants of India have been blamed because
they have not developed the cotton production as
that of other things, as though the special mission
of the Indian merchant was to have foreseen the
American blockade, and the policy of the European

powers,—in a word, to have ruined himself, in order to rescue Lancashire. Of course the Indian and Home Governments have been blamed by the manufacturers; the manufacturers have been blamed by everyone else, while nobody is really to be blamed, as nobody could have prevented the result which has taken place. The blockade has caused all the trouble, and its removal is the only remedy. The question, as regards India, has seldom been fairly stated. It is not whether India, by any possibility, can supply England with cotton, but whether she can supply it now, and of such a sort as England needs. Mr. Laing, the best authority who has yet spoken, has given a most decided negative in reply, and every fact yet adduced serves to confirm this view. Let us, however, admit the capacity of India to produce such cotton, and of such quantity as desired; will she make the endeavour as long as there is the least danger that the supplies in America may be brought into the market? India cannot afford to furnish her cotton, inferior as it is, in greatly increased quantities at former prices; and all the world knows that, should the supply from America commence to flow in, her cotton would have no chance, except in the ridiculous remedy of an import tax upon the cotton produced by slave labour. This would of course result in transferring the seat of cotton manufacture to the Continent. The estimates of the amount of cotton available for 1863 have been

much too large; but even admitting the correctness
of the figures of those who look ruin most hopefully
in the face, they do not represent the amount of
relief claimed from them. For the large amount of
manufactured goods on hand must cooperate with the
fear to manufacture inferior cotton, in hindering any
activity in the manufacture of Indian cottons, since
the doubt exists that, before the present supply of
goods is exhausted, an infinitely better class of cotton
will come into the market. Even the most hopeful
do not claim that the mill owners will be able to run
their mills with profit; but that they may do so
without loss. In considering the amount of cotton
to be expected, sufficient stress has not been laid
upon the fact, that great increase in price has drained
all cotton-growing countries of any reserve which
might have been on hand, so that we must depend
upon the crops now maturing or being gathered. The
fact that the Continent has heretofore used the greater
part of the cotton from India, would seem to indicate
that the increased supply will benefit it more than
England. An examination of all the facts which
bear upon the question of the cotton supply leads to
the conclusion that we cannot reckon upon the mills
working much more than an average of two days
full time during the coming year, should the
cotton of America be kept out of the market so long.
It may be a little more, and yet the ruinous effects

will be but slightly modified. After all, it is sounder economy to support the operatives than to clog the market with a superabundance of inferior cloth.

The other sources of supply, furnishing at present about 70,000,000 lbs., are generally admitted to be incapable of any very rapid extension. Considering the enormous interests at stake, it is a source for wonder that the subject of the cotton supply has been so imperfectly understood in England, and that in the agony of the present industrial convulsion any portion of the educated public should seek consolation in stupid ravings against the system of labour in the Southern States, or hope for relief for Lancashire from the almost unexplored and unorganized resources of Africa. It seems that, in their hatred of the South, these advocates of peace or extermination, according to the mood of the moment, have forgotten that the want is immediate, that fellow beings are suffering, that proud wills are being bent, and sensitive hearts broken, and that the grand question of commercial supremacy is involved; while they offer for hope a possibility not to be realized in a half century, if even in so short a space of time. Do these dreamers and excited missionaries believe that commerce can be revolutionised by a sample of cotton and a little platform notoriety? Has it not long been known that Africa produced cotton indigenously? Do these good people forget that Africa is the great

slaveholding country of modern times? Do they
forget that more slaves are used in Africa as human
sacrifices than are exported to the whole world
besides? Have they forgotten the King of Dahomey?
It seems that, instead of the present calamities
of England having been caused by the ' wickedness
of using slave-grown cotton,' they have resulted
rather from its scarcity.

In estimating the stock of cotton on hand in
America, the amount which must have been used
for home purposes during the war seems to have
been left out of question. Before the war commenced, the South manufactured cotton annually
to the amount of 185,000 bales, or 74,000,000 lbs.
Since the war, she could not have consumed in this
way less than 500,000 bales. Before the war the
Southern States were large importers of cotton goods,
those manufactured by her being of the heavier sorts.
Since the war, being cut off from her usual supply,
and being neither a cultivator of flax nor of wool to
any extent, she has been compelled to use cotton
goods as a substitute for goods manufactured from
those articles. The amount used as a substitute for
leather in the form of roping and coarse cloth must
have been very great, not to speak of that used for
tents, waggon-covers, and the like. Of course, a
considerable part of this will have been manufactured
by hand.

The rapidity with which the supply of American cotton could be brought forward upon the opening of the blockaded ports has, it seems, been exaggerated in both senses. The surplus of the crop of 1860, which is not unimportant, will in all probability have been packed, and, though retained in the interior, can be brought forward to the seaboard with rapidity. The exact time necessary for the shipowners to get information that it will be safe to send ships forward, for the latter to reach the Southern ports, load, and return to Liverpool, must depend upon whether steamers or sailing ships will be used in the first instance. On account of the high price of cotton, and the necessity for European manufactured articles in the South, it is highly probable that at first the number of steam-vessels bringing return cargoes of cotton will not be inconsiderable, and that, though there is no possibility of any large amount of American cotton being thrown upon the market at any one time, still some relief will be obtained from moderate supplies arriving shortly after the termination of the war. Those speculative interests which have been brought into existence by the blockade naturally seek to show that an opening of the ports would bring great disaster upon the country; yet this is unimportant, when compared with the injury which follows upon the existence of the blockade and the uncertainty of its termination.

There is no doubt that a much longer continuance of the blockade, or a serious disturbance of the labour system of the South, would be of permanent injury to the commercial position of England. The war will never be terminated by the surrender on the part of the South of the objects for which she fights; while the North has given every evidence of a savage determination to do her worst, regardless of the laws of justice, humanity, and of common decency, so that, whether in suspending all the rights of her own citizens, in the massacre of prisoners of war, in warring upon women, children, and defenceless men, in sacking and burning of towns, in exciting a half civilized race to the extermination of a civilized people, in gloating over the distress of Manchester, or in her forgetfulness of all the rules of intercourse between civilized nations, she but declares herself what she, by the composition and character of the majority of her people, truly is, a nation with all the appliances of civilization and the nature of savages.

We have seen that the consumption of East Indian cotton by Great Britain was only 176,000 bales, or about 56,700,000 lbs.; while the export trade to India in cotton yarns and cloths amounts to not far from 8,000,000*l.* annually. These, of course, must be mostly manufactured from American cotton, so that we may regard it as established that she has obtained this market by means of the large quantity, superior quality, and cheapness of American cotton. For a confirmation of this view we have but to consider that the Indian manufactures, primitive as they are, have held their ground tolerably well against the capital, machinery, and skill of Europe, and this leaves no ground for supposing that had England heretofore obtained her supply of cotton from India, her manufactures of cotton would have attained any great importance; and leads us to believe that, should the supply from America be long cut off or seriously diminished, she would be driven from some of her best markets. This applies with especial force to the Asiatic market, the grand field for the future extension of the consumption of cotton, which, once opened, would tax the producing power of the world to the utmost. I have, up to this point, purposely avoided referring to the distance of India from Europe as a source of disadvantage in the competition with America in furnishing the English market with raw cotton. This, though in that sense a disadvantage to India, would be, in case England lost the advantage which American cotton gives her, an important advantage for India in the manufacture of cotton, which might transfer the capital of Manchester to the banks of the Ganges. The chances of this would be much increased were a decided improvement in the staple of Indian cotton to take place,

thus, possibly, enabling her to compete with England
in all parts of the world, even should American
cotton continue to flow into the market. England
excels India only in capital, skilled labour, and cheap
coal; while the extreme cheapness of labour in India
(it being only a fourth so dear as in England), the
ingenious and docile nature of the inhabitants, the
superior climate for manufacturing purposes, and
the fact that the producer of the raw material, the
manufacturer and the consumer of manufactured
articles are upon the same spot, give India advantages
not to be despised. Cheap coal is not an advantage
of great importance; and the want of capital and
trained labour are by no means insurmountable
obstacles in the case of India. The extreme jealousy
of those interested in obtaining cotton from India
and extending the market there for cotton yarns and
cloths, because of the petty import duty of $3\frac{1}{2}$ and
5 per cent. upon these, will be a sufficient proof that
the question is not entirely a speculative one. It is
not uninteresting to observe, how entirely these persons regard India as 'clay in the hands of a potter.'
Surely, if it be true that the affair is so nicely
balanced, it would be a temptation, regarded from
the ' Indian point of view,' to neglect for a short
time the teachings of Adam Smith. Mr. Laing, in a
letter addressed to Samuel Giles, Hon. Sec. to the
Manchester Committee formed for the abolition of

the Indian tariff on cotton goods and yarns, writes as follows :

'The cotton industry is the largest branch of English manufactures, and India is the largest market in the world for cotton goods. India has also a large native manufacture, which, although conducted for the most part by primitive methods, still enters into effective competition with the imported article over a large area. India, moreover, is commencing cotton manufacture with all the advantages of modern science and machinery, under circumstances which hold out good hope of future progress.

'A cotton factory at Bombay has the advantage of saving two freights—on the raw material homewards, and the manufactured article outwards; and her labour, even now, after the great recent rise of wages in India, is at about the same rate per month as is paid per week in Lancashire. Coal is dearer, but this is a comparatively small item in the total cost of the production of a factory, and the main disadvantage is the want of that concentration of capital and skill which is found in a district which has been for years the metropolis of the cotton-manufacturing interest of the world. But this is a disadvantage which diminishes with the creation of every new factory, and, as regards the Indian market at least, the comparative cheapness of labour and raw material makes the rising factories of India rivals not to be despised.

'I admit, therefore, fully the importance, from an English point of view, of a further reduction of the 5 per cent. import duty. But if India is to be retained in peaceful and loyal allegiance to the British Crown, these matters must be looked upon in an Indian as in an English point of view; and the interests and wishes and the feelings of its 150,000,000 of inhabitants must be the primary consideration in deciding how to raise the necessary revenue.'

The same high authority has also said that 'our only hope is from America,' and the facts bearing on the case tend to confirm this idea; nor should the evidence of a citizen of the Confederate States be received with more suspicion, since the planters of the South fear no competition, and know that their interests for a long time to come will be identical with those of England. Cheerless, indeed, would be their feelings, should the termination of this war find the capital and labour of England now employed in the cotton trade scattered and disorganised. Concentrated in a small space, the sufferings of this vast interest must in England be tenfold more intense than in other countries, and the recovery will be comparatively slow. Circumstances have broken the effects of the blow upon the prosperity of England caused by the war in America; but should the supply of American cotton be much longer deferred, the chief advantage in the manufacture of cotton possessed by England over the Continental States will be lost.

Should the war not disorganise the labour of the South more than it has up to this time, there will be no diminution of importance in the supply of cotton which she will hereafter be able to furnish. Should no more of the cotton already gathered be destroyed, there will be, at least, as much on the plantations as would amount to a full crop; and should the war close before March 1, 1863, the crop for that year would not be so much diminished by the desolation of the plantations on the coast and rivers as might be thought, since the large excess of provisions in the country will enable the rest to cultivate a greater area in cotton.

The question of the future political relations of India might here be discussed; but this, though of great interest in connection with the cotton question, would lead us too far. It would be easy to show that, supposing India as capable of furnishing England with cotton as the Southern States, still, from political causes, this supply will be, in the future at least, equally liable to disturbance as that from the South.

The cotton trade of England, gigantic as it may seem, is small in comparison with what it may become, in case of the continued prosperity of the Southern States, as it is but in its infancy.

BOLLING A. POPE.

LONDON: *December* 1862.

THE SECOND WAR OF INDEPENDENCE
IN AMERICA.

CHAPTER I.

POLITICAL RELATIONS OF THE STATES OF THE UNION TO EACH OTHER.

THE first tendency of distinct communities in America to form political leagues is to be sought for at a period soon after the settlement of the colonies in New England, about the middle of the seventeenth century. As early as the year 1607 the English had planted a colony in Virginia, and a few years subsequently the Dutch one in New York. It was at a still later period that the English established themselves in the region afterwards known as New England.

The presence of the Dutch settlers in New York called forth a feeling of jealousy on the part of certain colonies of English origin, which caused them to conclude an offensive and defensive alliance,

B

to which they gave the name 'the United Colonies
of New England.'   An examination of the character
of this first confederation shows that its provisions
were limited to a state of war, to the relations of its
members with the Indians, and to the rendition of
fugitives from justice.   In all other respects the
jurisdiction and government of each colony was
reserved to itself.   On more than one occasion, it
may be remarked, did it occur that differences arose
about the construction of these simple Articles of
Union.*

From this it will appear that the sole motive for
union was self-defence; and it is singular to observe
that the provisions of this first confederation, in
substance, obtained a conspicuous place in the construction of the later American Union.

The second political league that claims our attention in America was that of all the English colonies
on the Atlantic coast, which was formed in compli-
ance with the recommendation of their delegates in
Congress assembled at Philadelphia in September
1774.

When the colonies sent their delegates to this
general Congress at Philadelphia, alleging that the
English Government had deprived them of a part of
their inalienable rights, there was no intention on

---

* Tucker : 'History of the United States.'   Philadelphia, 1856.
Vol. i. p. 29.

their part of revolting from the crown of England.
On the contrary, the sole design was to devise means
for obtaining redress of their different grievances.
To some of the delegates no instructions whatever
were given, except to attend the Congress. This
was true in the case of New Jersey and New York.

The chief ground of complaint was, notoriously,
the fact that taxes had been imposed upon the
colonies without their consent. It was contended
that in conformity to the English constitution, no
portion of the country could be taxed without being
represented, and that it was both unconstitutional
and unjust to deny to the colonies the right of sending representatives to the English parliament, or at
least of having a parliament of their own.

As a second cause of grievance was characterised
the infringement of the right of personal liberty
of the colonists; who instead of being tried
by peers of their own country, as other English
subjects, were transported to England, there to
answer to criminal accusations before foreign tri-
bunals.

Accordingly Congress made a declaration of the
fundamental rights of all the colonists, giving prominence to the right of trial by jury, and security of
personal liberty by means of the privilege of the writ
of habeas corpus.

It was only when it was ascertained that the

measures proposed by Congress, and the representations made to the Crown had failed to attain the intended results, that the colonies determined to dissolve all political connection with the mother country.

In their celebrated Declaration of Independence the colonists proclaimed that to their inalienable rights belong 'life, liberty, and the pursuit of happiness; that to secure these rights, governments are instituted among men, deriving their just powers from the consent of the governed.' Because these rights had been violated, the colonies threw off their allegiance to the crown.

When, however, England decided to force the colonies to obedience, they united, thirteen in number, for their common defence, to offer resistance; and thus commenced the *first war of independence in America.*

Authority for conducting the war, and for providing for the general welfare of the colonies, was delegated to the Congress of Philadelphia, known in American history as the ' Old Continental Congress.'

Conformably to these powers, certain ' Articles of Confederation' were framed and adopted by Congress, which were intended to serve as the conditions of a permanent union of the colonies. The ' Articles of Confederation' which had been adopted on November 15, 1777, by Congress, would never have obtained any legal validity or binding authority whatever, without the ratification of the individual colonies, as was expressly declared at that time. For in pursuance of a resolution of Congress the 'Articles of Confederation' were sent to the different* colonies, now styled States, for ratification, and were, at different times during the period between 1777 and 1781, successively ratified by the conventions of the several States.   In this act we perceive the first open recognition of the sovereignty claimed by the individual States.   That no doubt whatever may remain as to the existence of the claim of sovereignty by the States, and of their mutual recognition of their respective claims, it may be well to consider the provisions of the 'Articles of Confederation.'   We read as follows: —

'Art. II. Each State retains its sovereignty, freedom, and independence, and every power, jurisdiction, and right, which is not by this Confederation expressly delegated to the United States in Congress assembled.'

No room is here left for doubt.   Not only was the sovereignty of each State acknowledged by all the others, but, by the unequivocal terms of this league, this sovereignty was emphatically reserved to the States.

In the meantime, between 1776 and 1780, each of

* Tucker, vol. i. p. 225.

the thirteen States, with the exception of New Jersey
and Connecticut, which still retained the charters
granted by Charles II. in 1662, had framed a new
constitution. And, with the exception of Massachusetts alone, every State had adopted its new
constitution before the framing of the 'Articles of
Confederation' by the Old Congress. We know, in
fact, that the constitutions of the States served in a
measure as a model for the 'Articles of Confederation.'
And as the States asserted their sovereignty, in their
constitutions, prior to the adoption of the 'Articles
of Confederation,' it cannot be maintained that the
States derived their sovereignty from the Union.

A clear notion of the nature of this league may be
gained by a further examination of the provisions of
the 'Articles of Confederation.' The objects of the
league are stated as follows : — 'Art. III. The said
States hereby severally enter into a firm league of
friendship with each other, for their common defence,
the security of their liberties, and their mutual and
general welfare ; binding themselves to assist each
other against all force offered to or attacks made upon
them or any of them.'

Is it not evident from this language that, at least
here, there was no idea of a consolidated government
ignoring the sovereignty of the single States ?

For the better management of the general interests
of the United States, a Congress is provided by

Art. V. whose powers are subsequently enumerated with the greatest care.

Finally, it is provided by Art. XIII. that 'Every State shall abide by the determination of the United States in Congress assembled, in all questions which by this Confederation are submitted to them. And the articles of this Confederation shall be inviolably observed by every State, and the Union shall be perpetual: nor shall any alterations at any time hereafter be made in them, unless such alteration be agreed to in a Congress of the United States, and be afterwards confirmed by the legislatures of every State.'

The most convincing evidence of the weakness of the Federal Government under the 'Articles of Confederation' is the total absence of any provision for enforcing the execution of its own laws. Not one word occurs with reference to this subject in that instrument. Nor can it be assumed that this power was to be *inferred*, for the Federal Government possessed no powers but such as were 'expressly delegated to it,' as we have seen in Art. II. We agree entirely with the distinguished statesman who asserts that the Federal Government was 'destitute of even the shadow of constitutional power to enforce the execution of its own laws.' * The reason of this seems

* See No. xxi. of the 'Federalist'— a collection of essays written in favour of the new constitution. New York 1788. No better authority for the interpretation of the constitution is to be found than the 'Federalist.'

obvious.   It was the intention of the States, in unit-
ing under the ' Articles of Confederation,' to secure
themselves against external attacks.   No doubt was
entertained that in the presence of a common danger
they would be induced to cooperate with accord for
self-defence.   This being then the chief object of the
league, it was held to be unnecessary to grant any
special power to the Federal Government for that
purpose ; particularly when such power might tend
to restrict the exercise of certain rights based upon
the sovereignty of the States.   In fact, nothing was
more natural than that in attempting to make themselves independent of the English Government, the
States should have been chary of constituting a government at home, with powers which might be used for
oppressing themselves.   We shall see, however, that
the provisions of this league were for the most part
continued in the ' Constitution ' which was framed
to replace it.

Experience soon demonstrated that the ' Articles
of Confederation ' were sufficient neither for the
administration of the general interests, nor for
promoting the general welfare of the States,
owing to their conflicting interests.   In a word, the
means were not adequate to the accomplishment of
the object proposed; consequently, the Government
soon fell into decay, no one seemed to take any
interest in its success.   To remedy these glaring

defects in the Federal Government, delegates were
sent from twelve of the thirteen States, Rhode Island
refusing to participate, to a general convention,
which assembled in Philadelphia in May 1787, to
consult and devise measures for rendering the Union
'more perfect.' In this convention, which was pre-
sided over by Washington, efforts were made to
define more exactly the relations of the States to
each other, as well as to their general agent, the
Federal Government. The most important task,
however, was to remove for the future those causes
for contention, which had in more than one instance
already jeopardised the peace of the country. By
reconciling conflicting interests it was hoped to
attain this result. It is evident that this was an
undertaking of no little magnitude. For the
population and extent of the several States was a
fruitful cause of dispute with reference to the basis
of representation, as well as the varied geographical
situations, which gave rise to oft recurring difficulties.

Commercial intercourse also was a source of
bitter discord. The States possessing harbours and
the facilities for trade in ships found it to their
interest to exclude foreign shipping from competition
with their own. On the other hand, those States
which were less fortunate in this respect discerned in
the exclusion of foreign ships a decided disadvantage
for themselves, because competition would have had

the effect of rendering the importation of foreign articles cheaper. These States demanded the removal of the restrictions against competition. To this the shipping States replied by refusing to accede to any diminution of their advantages without full indemnity. An appeal was also made to the patriotism of all the States to permit a policy which would result in creating a navy for the United States, the want of which had been felt so severely during the war.

Finally, after long and tedious deliberations, on September 17, 1787, the convention adopted a new constitution which was communicated to Congress. The constitution having met with the approval of Congress, was, in conformity with a resolution of that body, sent to the States to be ratified or rejected by their conventions. As will be seen from the table below, nearly three years elapsed before the constitution obtained the ratification of all the States.*

---

* The constitution was ratified by the State conventions in the following order :—

Delaware	on	.	.	December 7, 1787.
Pennsylvania	.	.	.	December 12, 1787.
New Jersey	.	.	.	December 18, 1787.
Georgia	.	.	.	January 2, 1788.
Connecticut	.	.	.	January 9, 1788.
Massachusetts	.	.	.	February 6, 1788.
Maryland	.	.	.	April 28, 1788.
South Carolina	.	.	.	May 23, 1788.
New Hampshire	.	.	.	June 21, 1788.
Virginia	.	.	.	June 26, 1788.
New York	.	.	.	July 26, 1788.
North Carolina	.	.	.	November 21, 1789.
Rhode Island	.	.	.	May 29, 1790.

Before entering upon a detailed examination of the new constitution, it is necessary to contrast one of its articles with one of the 'Articles of Confederation.' Art. VII. of the 'Constitution' reads as follows:—

'The ratification of the conventions of nine States shall be sufficient for the establishment of this constitution between the States so ratifying the same.'

We find the following words in Art. XIII. of the 'Articles of Confederation':—

'And the Articles of the Confederation shall be inviolably observed by every State, and the Union shall be perpetual; nor shall any alteration at any time hereafter be made in any of them, unless such alteration be agreed to in a Congress of the United States, and be afterwards confirmed by the legislatures of every State.'

If we are to interpret the language of Art. XIII. of the 'Articles of Confederation' literally, we must arrive at the conclusion that the theory of those who contend that the Union was a thing which could never constitutionally cease to exist, is devoid of all foundation in fact, and eminently absurd. For it is provided by this article, that any alteration may be made to the 'Articles of Confederation' by obtaining the consent of 'the legislatures of every State.' And as no prominence over the other articles is given to that provision which declares that 'the

Union shall be perpetual,' the conclusion is inevitable that, under one condition at least, the *unanimous* consent of all the States, that provision might be cancelled, and the Union would be at an end.

But we must not stop here. How are the facts to be accounted for, that in direct contradiction to Art. XIII. just cited, the new constitution in **Art. VII.** declares that not the *unanimous* consent of all the States, but simply the ratification of *nine* States, should be sufficient for dissolving the Union? Unquestionably, the notion of individual consent on the part of the States lies at the foundation of it. The fundamental idea that the 'Articles of Confederation' constituted a treaty, and nothing more, between independent and sovereign States, was firmly established in the convictions of the people. And it was believed here too that, as in the case of treaties generally, a breach of one article is a breach of the whole treaty, and in this case, one party to the treaty failing in its obligations, the others are left free to consider themselves liberated altogether from the compact. Indeed, one of the able commentators in the 'Federalist'* confirms this view. He says:—

'Should it unhappily be necessary to appeal to these delicate truths (i.e. the principles regarding treaties just enunciated) for a justification for dispensing with the consent of particular States to a dissolution

* Federalist, No. xliii.

of the federal pact, will not the complaining party
find it a difficult task to answer the *multiplied* and
important infractions with which they may be con-
fronted?'

Is not this language sufficiently unequivocal?
Here the right of *nine* States to dissolve the Union is
assumed as self-evident, by reason of their sovereignty;
but, to avoid all appearance of illegality, the right is
further based upon that most general principle of
treaties between foreign nations. These are the
words of an eminent advocate of the new constitution, to prove that there was nothing unconstitutional
in disregarding Art. XIII. of the 'Articles of Confederation.'

Facts show that in practice, at least, this doctrine
was fully recognised. By reference to the dates of
the ratification of the constitution by the conventions
of the States, it will be seen that the first secession
from the Union took place on the part of Delaware,
on December 7, 1787. Successively eight States
more seceded, till on June 21, 1788, nine States
having given their adhesion to the constitution as
required, a new Union came into existence. But
there was left the old Union, consisting of the States
of Virginia, New York, North Carolina, and Rhode
Island. Subsequently three of these States seceded
to the New Union, and so Rhode Island was left
alone, and did exist for six months and six days as

an independent sovereign State, in no way constitutionally bound to the ' United States.'

From May 29, 1790, however, the new Union consisted of all the thirteen original States, and the constitution was in force among them all.

A general idea of the constitution may be gained from the following summary of its provisions. The words of the preamble express distinctly the objects for which the constitution was framed. These are ' to form a more perfect Union, establish justice, ensure domestic tranquillity, provide for the common defence, promote the general welfare, and secure the blessings of liberty to ourselves and our posterity.'

Art. I. establishes a Congress, to which certain powers are delegated, they being most carefully and accurately enumerated.

Art. II. provides for the office and duties of the executive, whilst it expressly designates the authority and extent of authority conferred upon the President.

Art. III. regulates the judiciary of the United States.

Art. IV. defines more exactly certain relations of the States to each other, as also to their general agent, the Federal Government.

Art. V. relates exclusively to the manner of amending the constitution.

Art. VI. acknowledges the validity of certain

claims against the old confederation, and charac-
terises the constitution as the supreme law of the
land, and requires certain officers of the States as
well as of the United States to be bound by oath or
affirmation to support the constitution.

Art. VII. makes the validity of the constitution
depend upon the consent of each individual State.

Two points of difference between the 'Articles of
Confederation' and the constitution suggest themselves at the first glance. Firstly, among the
enumerated powers of Congress, that of making laws
to carry into execution all powers vested in the
Federal Government by the constitution. Experience
had taught the people of the States that such power
was necessary for the Federal Government. Nor was
there anything repulsive in the idea of it. On
entering into this new league, it was but reasonable
that the States should consent, and desire to have the
terms of the pact fulfilled.

This was both wise and just. It would have been
preposterous for a State, having entered into the
Union under certain conditions, to have allowed these
conditions to be violated by its citizens, whilst remaining a party to the league. As might naturally
have been supposed, the power to act upon *individuals
directly* was accorded to the Federal Government, as
being the most practicable and most expedient
way of enforcing observance of the constitution.

This was too a matter of convenience for the States generally.

Secondly, we miss in the constitution that clause of the 'Articles of Confederation' which provides that 'each State retains its sovereignty, freedom, and independence; and every power, jurisdiction, and right, which is not, by this confederation, expressly delegated to the United States in Congress assembled.'

Can any misconception arise from this omission? We think not. No declaration of independence or sovereignty was needed. This had been achieved by the war with England. Equally self-evident was it, that none but *delegated* powers could appertain to the Federal Government. The Federal Government was the creature of the State-sovereignties, and could only possess attributes conferred by these States. Gradually, however, a party sprang into existence which advocated a consolidated general government, and desired to see this centralised at the expense of State-sovereignty, State-rights. Short-lived as was this party, the *Federalists*, it succeeded in arousing the fears of the States, lest the Federal Government should assume powers not belonging to it. The result was that about six months after the Constitution had gone into operation, this reservation of non-delegated powers was expressly declared in Amendment X. to the Constitution.*

* Immediately after the meeting of the first Congress, the amendments to the Constitution were passed with the following preamble :—

Upon consideration it appears that the intention in forming the constitution, was not to make an organic change in the nature of the Federal Government. It was to alter and revise the 'Articles of Confederations' that the delegates assembled in Congress at Philadelphia. To revivify and give efficacy to the existing conditions of Union, rather than to make new ones, was the object of the constitution.

Without doubt, the best exponents of the constitution were its framers; for the intention of the law-giver is the law, as we know from the universal maxims of jurisprudence. None among these is entitled to as much respect as James Madison. At the time when it was proposed to ratify the constitution, a series of essays were published by the most eminent statesmen of the time to ensure this result. In these we have happily the opinions of those very men, whose energy and ability produced the constitution. Perhaps nothing contributed more to the adoption of the constitution than the writings of Hamilton, Madison, and Jay, which we now possess in the 'Federalist.' Here we have the opinions of

'The Conventions of a number of States having, at the time of their adopting the constitution, expressed a desire, in order to prevent misconstruction or abuse of its powers, that further declaratory and restrictive clauses should be added; and as extending the ground of public confidence in the government will best insure the beneficent ends of its institutions, therefore, Resolved, &c.'

both parties of that period, all agreeing in regard to the nature of the Federal Government under the constitution.

By reference to the recorded opinions of Madison,* a clear and unprejudiced view of this question may be obtained. In explaining the nature of the Federal Government, he says :—

' The proposed constitution, therefore, when tested by the rules laid down by its antagonists, is, in strictness, neither a national nor a Federal constitution, but a composition of both. In its *foundation* it is Federal, not national; in the *sources* from which the ordinary powers of government are drawn, it is partly Federal and partly national; in the *operation* of these powers, it is national not Federal; in the *extent* of them, again, it is Federal not national; and, finally, in the authoritative mode of introducing amendments, it is neither wholly Federal nor wholly national.'

As to its foundation, Madison lucidly demonstrates that the constitution is *Federal.* He remarks : —

' On examining the first relation, it appears on one hand that the constitution is to be founded on the assent and ratification of the people of America, given by deputies elected for the special purpose; but, on the other hand, that this assent and ratification is to be given by the people, not as individuals composing

* Federalist, No. xxxix.

one entire nation, but as composing the distinct and independent States to which they respectively belong. It is to be the assent and ratification, of the several States derived from the supreme authority in each State, the authority of the people themselves. The act, therefore, establishing the constitution, will not be a *national* but a *Federal* act.'

In support of this Madison urges further, that 'it is to result neither from a decision of a *majority* of the people of the Union, nor from that of a *majority* of the States; it must result from the *unanimous* assent of the several States that are parties to it, differing in no otherwise from their ordinary assent than in its being expressed, not by the legislative authority, but that of the people themselves.' But we know that according to the American theory of self-government, as enunciated in the Declaration of Independence, ' the right of the people to alter or abolish' any form of government, ' and to institute a new government,' is asserted to be *incontestable*. Now we have the explicit declaration of Madison to the effect, that the assent given to the constitution differed in nowise from the ordinary assent than in the manner of its expression by the people *directly* through a convention. Hence we deduce that, in assenting to the constitution, the States did no act prejudicial to this right to withdraw their consent whenever it should be deemed expedient.

Nevertheless, the 'Father of the Constitution' does not desert us here. He informs us that:

'Each State in ratifying the constitution is considered as a sovereign body independent of all others, and only to be bound by its own voluntary act. In this relation then the new constitution will, if established, be a *Federal* and not a national constitution.'

With regard to the 'sources from which the ordinary powers of government are to be derived,' Madison describes the constitution as a complex. For he continues:

'The House of Representatives will derive its powers from the people of America, and the people will be represented in the same proportion and on the same principle as they are in the legislature of a particular State.' Whilst the 'Senate, on the other hand, would derive its powers from the States, as political and co-equal sovereignties; and these will be represented on the principle of equality in the Senate, as they now are in the existing Congress.' The election of the President is also complex. 'From this aspect of the government, it appears to be of a mixed character, presenting at least as many *Federal* as *national* features.'

The *operation* of the powers of the constitution is 'national,' says Madison, 'though perhaps not so completely as has been understood. In several cases, and particularly in the trial of controversies to which the States may be parties, they must be viewed and proceeded against in their collective or political capacities only.'

Unquestionably reference is here made to the way of acting upon individuals in a State directly by the Federal Government. This, as we have seen, does not, however, impair the sovereignty of the States in the least.

Madison proceeds as follows:

'But if the government be national with regard to the operation of its powers, it changes its aspect again when we contemplate it in relation to the *extent* of its powers. The idea of a national government involves in itself not only an authority over the individual citizens, but an indefinite supremacy over all persons and things, so far as they are objects of lawful government. Among a people consolidated into one nation this supremacy is completely vested in the national legislature. Among communities united for particular purposes, it is vested partly in the general and partly in the municipal legislatures. In the former case, all local authorities are subordinate to the supreme; and may be controuled, directed, or abolished by it at pleasure. In the latter, the local or municipal authorities form distinct and independent portions of the supremacy, no more subject, within their respective spheres, to the general authority, than the general authority is subject to them within its own sphere. In this relation, then, the proposed government can not be a *national* one, since its jurisdiction extends to certain enumerated objects only, and leaves to the States a residuary and inviolable sovereignty over all other objects.'

Here we have the essence of the whole matter. Supremacy is a necessity of a national government, and this supremacy is founded upon sovereignty. One cannot exist without the other. The Federal Government, as it is seen, possesses neither of them; its jurisdiction is limited to 'certain enumerated objects only,' and does not at all infringe the sovereignty of the individual States, which is *inviolable*.

Amendments to the constitution are said by Madison to be both Federal and national, because of the number of State votes necessary to ratify and make an amendment a part of the constitution. Not the unanimous ratification of all the States, but only that of three-fourths, at that time ten, was required, and hence it appeared as though the adoption of an amendment had somewhat the character of a national act. This is, however, only apparent, not real. For in agreeing to the constitution unanimously, the State agreed to this rule of action for the future. They bound themselves voluntarily to be governed in a certain event by the

decision of three-fourths of their number, just in the
same manner as they agreed, in Sect. V. of Art. 1 of
the Constitution, that 'a majority of each (House)
shall constitute a quorum to do business.' Here,
however, the matter is decided by votes of *States*, not
of a majority of three-fourths of the people.   In a
word, this provision of the constitution in nowise
lessened the sovereignty of the States.

Summing up these considerations, it appears that
in the two most vital points of the Federal constitution, its *foundation* and the *extent of its powers*, it is
purely Federal, having no characteristics of nationality
whatever.   That in two other respects, less important
in themselves, in the *sources* of the ordinary powers
of government, and the *operation* of these powers,
there is a mixture of both, though the Federal
features predominate largely in the former, on account
of the Senate.   That with regard to amendments, the
constitution is only apparently national, but in truth
Federal, and not at all derogatory of the sovereignty
of the States.

This testimony of Madison is sufficient to remove
every doubt as to the nature of the Union, and to
establish conclusively the principle of State sovereignty.

But in the fact that even after the ratification of
the constitution by the unanimous votes of all the
States, it was indispensable to obtain the ratification

of amendments to the constitution from the States in
their sovereign capacity, and not from the inhabitants
at large, we perceive the continued existence of the
sovereignty of the individual States.   Two years after
the constitution had been confirmed by all of the
States, twelve amendments were proposed in the prescribed manner, but only ten of them having been
confirmed by the States, these only became integral
parts of the constitution.   Furthermore, these ten
amendments were *restrictions of the powers of the
Federal Government, or supplementary means of protection for the rights of the States, or of individuals,
and evinced the characteristic political jealousy towards
the Federal Government*—a striking proof for the refu-
tation of the arguments of those who assert, that by
adopting a new constitution the thirteen original
States made a surrender of their sovereignty to the
Federal Government.

In Art. X. of the Amendments to the Constitution,
we read furthermore: ' *The powers not delegated to the
United States by the Constitution, nor prohibited by it to
the States, are reserved to the States respectively, or to
the people.*'   From this it follows, as before intimated,
that here, as well as under the ' Articles of Confederation,' the United States possessed no powers but
such as were delegated by the States.

Some partisans of the Union have asserted that, by
the expression ' *or to the people,*' the idea is to be

conveyed that the inhabitants of the United States
constituted politically one sovereign people. For this
assumption there is not the slightest foundation in
fact.   Evidently, reference is here made to the two
ways in which a State may exercise its functions of
sovereignty.   The one through the legislature, here
termed the ' State,' the other by the voice of a ' State
convention,' designated above as ' the people.'   Were
further proof that the citizens of the several States,
taken in their totality, never have constituted one
people in the history of America, necessary, we should
refer again to the unequivocal declarations of Madison,
to the effect that—'The assent and ratification of the
people of America was given to the constitution,
*not as individuals comprising one entire nation, but as
composing the distinct and independent States to which
they respectively belong.'*   By referring to a similar
clause in the constitution of the Confederate States,
we find this idea fully expressed as follows:—

Art. VI. No. 6.   'The powers not delegated to
the Confederate States by the constitution, nor
prohibited by it to the States, are reserved to the
States respectively, *or to the people thereof.'*

In face of all that has been stated, it may be that still
other evidence of the sovereignty of the States may be
demanded.   If so, we refer to the history of those
times, and to the debates in the Convention which
framed the constitution, as also to the press of that

period. Whoever reads the debates in the Convention and in the Congress of 1787 must be impressed with the oft-recurring threats of dissolution of the Union, a circumstance which attracted little notice at that time, because no doubt whatever was entertained by anyone of the strictly constitutional right of a State to recall its delegated authority.

Even at this period some few statesmen were found who were desirous of circumscribing the sovereignty of the individual States, and of constituting a consolidated national government. Prominent amongst these were King of Massachusetts, Wilson of Pennsylvania, and Alexander Hamilton. Wilson and his colleagues advocated a representation of the States in the Senate, as well as in the House of Representatives, upon the basis of population exclusively; their proposal in the Convention was lost by a large majority of voices. And it was decided to the contrary that each State, without reference to extent or population, should send an equal number of representatives to the United States Senate. A proof that the interests of each individual State, represented in a union of States, should enjoy a perfect equality in its relations to the whole, and that consequently the individuality of each State, even in affairs entrusted to the administration of Congress, must be considered as existing unimpaired. This individuality has its origin and foundation in the sovereignty of the individual States, and can exist only so long as the sovereignty is complete. In accordance with this provision of the constitution, Delaware, with a population of 112,218 souls, has two votes in the United States Senate, whereas New York, with 3,887,542 inhabitants, is only entitled to the same number of votes in that branch of Congress. In this case, as on all occasions where it has been found necessary to decide between consolidation and State sovereignty, the latter has triumphed by forcing population into the background.

It is well known with what warmth the advocates of the Union in the Northern States have pressed everything approaching to an argument, to show their enmity to the doctrine of State rights. Among the principal grounds of their objections is the supposition, that a Federal Government based upon the principle of State sovereignty, as claimed by the Southern States, would be preposterous, irreconcilable with the notion of a durable government, and would contain the seeds of its own destruction within itself. Before questioning the claims of this species of argument to consideration, we desire to correct an error into which the feelings or inclinations of some men not unfrequently lead them. Obviously, it is altogether foreign to the question to state that a given condition of things never could have existed, because such a state of things is in opposition to our own convictions or notions of what is best at the present moment. In

examining the bearings of the question of State sovereignty, and the application of this notion to the construction of the Federal Government in the constitution, it is absolutely necessary to restrict our enquiries
to facts. Whether or not this principle, when applied
to the organization of government, is, in itself, and
abstractly, pernicious, is something with which we
are here in no way concerned. But we must endeavour
to decide this political problem: Was the idea of
State sovereignty the fundamental principle upon
which the Union was constructed? Did this continue
to be that principle which imparted to the constitution the moral and political force that bound the
States together up to the dissolution of the Union?
Both of these interrogatories must, as we have tried to
demonstrate, be answered affirmatively. This conceded, men may amuse or perplex themselves as much
as they like by devising universal theories of government, and though they should divest their ideas of all
reality in pursuit of their abstractions, it will not
affect the weight attaching to the opinions of such
men as the framers of the constitution. But before
leaving this subject altogether, one thought suggests
itself. It was proposed to form a government of the
thirteen States for their common defence. Each State
was sovereign. No community of interests existed
between many of them, except that resulting from
their weakness in the presence of a common danger.

Was it, then, to be expected, that these States differing so widely from each other would ever voluntarily have surrendered their most cherished rights, and have consolidated themselves into one central government, in which the bonds of Union would have been more galling because compulsory? Was it not rather an evidence of wise foresight on the part of the framers of the constitution, to have constructed the Union on the recognised principle of consent? Evidently it was believed that in leaving each State free to withdraw from the Union at pleasure, the States would be induced to make greater concessions to each other for the sake of preserving the Union and its benefits, and that in this way a stronger feeling of respect would be engendered, and a greater sense of justice and fairness would influence the States in their relations to each other. Above all, however, there was one excellency in this system of government. It provided for a peaceful separation of the States, whenever experience should demonstrate the continuance of the Union to be no longer desirable, or possible. How wise it would have been, had their descendants have executed the intentions of the authors of the constitution.

Another argument often advanced to show the inexpediency or absurdity of State sovereignty is the following: Were the right of a State to secede from the Union allowed, the right of a county to secede

from a State could not be denied. Much trouble
has been taken to deceive the people of Europe by
means of this fallacy. And we are sorry to confess
that it has not been ineffectual in deceiving quite a
number. No plausibility, however, atttaches to
this fallacy. It is well known that these counties
are only sub-divisions of the State territory and
population, existing for the more convenient administration of the laws. At pleasure the legislatures may,
and constantly do, change, unite or divide such
counties, or even merge them entirely into others.
These territorial divisions of a State have no political
existence or individuality whatever, and have no
historical foundation at all, upon which to base a
pretension to any of the rights of an independent,
sovereign community. Besides, who has ever heard
of such a claim being advanced by a county in any of
the States? It is simply absurd to institute such a
comparison between the States and the counties
thereof.

Others, again, maintain that the sovereignty of the
individual States is only a *limited* sovereignty. This
assumption is devoid of even the shadow of reason.
For sovereignty resides in the people of each State;
it is indivisible and incapable of restriction. And
the source of the rights of sovereignty which are
inherent in the people of the States, and inviolable,
remained unimpaired by the *delegation of the exercise*

of certain powers to the Union. Moreover, this *delegation*, which, as already stated, was accompanied by no *renunciation of the right of retraction*, could not under any circumstances signify more than the legal relation of a principal to his agent. On this point the testimony of Madison, already cited, is conclusive, and no other evidence is required to refute this objection.

Turning to the terms of recognition of the United States after the war of independence, on the part of Great Britain, the most explicit *acknowledgement* is made of the 'free, sovereign, and independent States,' the original thirteen being enumerated. France and the other European States, as well as Great Britain, all made treaties with the thirteen States in their individual sovereign capacity, in all of which treaties the States are designated by name.

From all that has been stated we now conclude that the Union possessed only the *exercise* of those powers which were expressly *delegated* to it; that the political individuality (sovereignty) remained intact to the separate States; that the States could have lost their sovereignty only by *express* surrender and abandonment of it; and that an express renunciation of the right to separate from the Union would in all cases have been necessary, in order to deprive the States of this inherent, natural right.

No one has ever denied that it was the desire and

intention of the framers of the constitution to render the Union as durable as possible ; but this desire had its foundation most certainly in the objects for which the Union was formed—' to establish justice, insure domestic tranquillity, provide for the common defence, promote the general welfare, and secure the blessings of liberty.' The Union was not its own object. In a word, the Union was intended to be the *means* of securing the objects above enumerated, and not to be the purpose of its own existence.

In recent times several States have seen fit to withdraw the delegation made to the Union of the exercise of certain powers, convinced that not the promotion of their welfare, but their injury, resulted from the policy pursued by the Union. In doing this, they did only what every constituent is competent to do. They withdrew a mandate which in public law, as in the civil law, is a contract that can exist only so long as the consent is mutual. And so they dissolved with full authority a league which had existed up to that time. By this act they did not repudiate the liabilities incurred by the whole, during their participation in the league, which they were still bound to fulfill according to the well-known rules of law respecting contracts between principal and agent. This they declared themselves ready to do, immediately upon their secession from the Union.

Advocates of the doctrine of secession, as an incontestable constitutional right, have not been confined to the Southern States. Ever since the establishment of the Union this right has been admitted by the great majority of the people in every State. Statesmen, politicians, and jurists have alike proclaimed secession to be a right under the constitution. It is only in recent times, since the 'Republican Party' which elected Mr. Lincoln has come into power, and since the withdrawal of the Southern States from the Union, that the right of secession has been questioned.

William Rawle, an authority of eminence, and at one time Attorney-General of the State of Pennsylvania, has left us his views upon the constitutionality of secession recorded in a work on the constitution. He remarks: *

'If a faction should attempt to subvert the government of a State for the purpose of destroying its Republican form, the paternal power of the Union could thus be called forth to subdue it. Yet it is not to be understood that its interposition would be justifiable, if the people of a State should determine to retire from the Union, whether they adopted another or retained the same form of government, or if they should, with the express intention of seceding,

---

* A View of the Constitution of the United States of America. By William Rawle, Philadelphia, 1825, p. 289.

D

expunge the representative system from their code, and thereby incapacitate themselves from concurring, according to the mode now prescribed, in the choice of certain public officers of the United States. . .
It depends on the State itself to retain or abolish the principle of representation, because it depends on itself whether it will continue a member of the Union. To deny this right would be inconsistent with the principle on which all our political systems are founded, which is, that the people have in all cases a right to determine how they will be governed.'

The same authority continues: *

'If the majority of the people of a State deliberately and peaceably resolve to relinquish the Republican form of government, they cease to be members of the Union. If a faction, an inferior number, make such an effort and endeavour to enforce it by violence, the case provided for will have arisen, and the Union is bound to employ its powers to prevent it.'

Without stopping to enquire whether a faction may not consist of a majority of the people of a State, it is obvious that the authority of Rawle overthrows the assertions of those who contend that the Union, having been formed by the unanimous consent of all the States, can only be dissolved by the unanimous consent of the same. But this argument

* William Rawle, loco citato, p. 292.

bears its contradiction on its own face. If it is true that the States did unanimously assent to the constitution, it is not the less certain that each State gave its adherence without reference to the others, and that, had the number of assenting States not exceeded nine, the Union would have existed for this number. And by the same process of reasoning it would appear that, should one or more States retire from the Union, their action would not affect the union of the other States, but the union would be dissolved only between the seceding State or States and the rest, not, however, between all the States. The action of any one State could in this case be binding only on itself. On this point Rawle is quite clear.[*]

'Secessions may reduce the number to the smallest integer admitting combination. They would remain united under the same principles and regulations among themselves that now apply to the whole. For a State cannot be compelled by other States to withdraw from the Union; and therefore, if two or more determine to remain united, although all the others desert them, nothing can be discovered in the constitution to prevent it.'

The same statesman observes at another place:[†]

'The secession of a State from the Union depends on the will of the people of such State. The people

[*] William Rawle, l. c. p. 299.   [†] Ibid. p. 295.

alone, as we have already seen, hold the power to alter their constitution.'

In confirmation of our statement, that the right of secession was generally admitted, we shall quote again the words of the Attorney-General of Pennsylvania. He says: *

'It was foreseen that there would be a natural tendency to increase the number of States with the anticipated increase of population, now so fully verified. It was also known, though it was not avowed, that a State might withdraw itself.'

No doubt now remaining as to the constitutional right of a State to separate from the Union, it remains to be seen how this separation may be effected. Unquestionably, the action terminating the connection of a State with the Union must be the action of the people of that State. In assenting to the constitution, a convention in each State, specially chosen by the people directly for that purpose, gave expression to the will of the people. The action of such a convention is binding, even above the laws of the State; for it has the highest sanctity of law possible, being the direct expression of the sovereign will of the people. Such action is final, and admits of no appeal. And if the resolution of a convention so constituted was sufficient for assenting to the constitution, it follows that a convention would be the proper organ through

* William Rawle, l. c. p. 297.

which the people should express their determination of withdrawing their assent to the constitution. Once more let us see what Rawle says on this subject: *

'But in any manner by which a secession is to take place, nothing is more certain than that the act should be deliberate, clear, unequivocal. The perspicuity and solemnity of the original obligation require correspondent qualities in its dissolution. The powers of the General Government cannot be defeated or impaired by an ambiguous or implied secession on the part of the State, although a secession may perhaps be conditional.'

By reference to the ordinances of secession of those States at present constituting the Confederate States, it will be seen that, so far from there having been less solemnity in the acts of their conventions, there was perhaps more than at the time of the adoption of the constitution. The formalities observed were not less striking, and the acts were not hasty, but the calm expression of the decided will of the people of these States. From this side, then, no objections can be urged against the constitutional validity of the secession of the Southern States.

And now, turning to the past, we shall see that steps had been taken as early as 1815, preliminary to secession on the part of five of the New England States, Maine forming the exception. The action of

* William Rawle, l. c. p. 296.

the Hartford Convention is proof of this allegation. For, although the proceedings of that body were to a great extent kept secret, it is now known that a resolution was passed to the effect that no further contributions of means for carrying on the war with Great Britain should be allowed by these States, and that no further contingents in troops should be sent beyond their borders. At the same time a demand was ordered to be made upon the General Government to put an end to the war, or, that failing, a secession was to be intimated as the eventual consequence.

For the rest, that State, which is now so loud in its denunciations of the secession of the Southern States, because its own material interests are at stake — I mean Massachusetts — was the most disloyal of the five New England States in 1815, and was the first which sent commissioners to the Federal Government at Washington to enforce the measures recommended by the Hartford Convention. Moreover, on two other occasions has this same State threatened to secede from the Union. We refer to the action of Massachusetts on the admission of Louisiana into the Union and on the annexation of Texas.

Is it not, then, an indication of the weakness of the cause of the opposite party to stigmatise as revolution, rebellion, or treason, that which others demonstrate to be a sacred constitutional right, especially when no evidence whatever has been adduced to invalidate the claim to this right?

CHAPTER II.

CAUSES OF THE DISSOLUTION OF THE UNION.

I. *Social Causes.*

In the previous chapter we have endeavoured to show from the early history of the colonies that the principle of State sovereignty was the fundamental notion upon which the Union was based.

To discover the first causes of the dissolution of the Union, it is necessary to go back still farther, to the history of the colonists before their emigration to America.

The first permanent settlement in America was that made in Virginia under a Royal Charter. As early as the year 1619, we find a legislative assembly existing there, which was formed after the model of the English Parliament. The King was represented by the Governor, the House of Lords by the council of the Governor, and the House of Commons by the House of Burgesses.* Accordingly Virginia was, in the strictest sense, a royal province, colonised by subjects

* Tucker, vol. i. p. 24.

of the English Crown, who evinced their attachment to the political institutions of the mother-country and their loyalty to the Crown by the organisation of their colonial Government and the adoption of the Anglican Church. Herein is a striking proof exhibited that the settlers of Virginia belonged to the Conservative party of England. Not the less true is it that they were among the most devoted adherents of royalty and the most steadfast friends of Charles I., who was executed in the course of the civil war.

When Cromwell became successful in England, a large number of the noblest cavaliers of Charles I. fled to Virginia. By the accession of these cavaliers, the population of the existing colony of Virginia was considerably increased. And it is well known that most of the Southern States were peopled by emigration from Virginia, and not by direct emigration from Europe. A congenial population was then already present in America to receive the Huguenots on their arrival. Such was the origin of the population of the Southern States.

Between 1605 and 1610, a religious sect left its English home, self-exiled, to seek in Holland religious freedom, and to escape persecution on account of its religious creed. In the year 1620, about one hundred of this religious sect, the *Puritans*, embarking at Leyden in Holland, landed in America on the inhospitable shores of Plymouth. These persons were mere adventurers, who had no right to the soil, much less a charter authorising them to organise a government. Nevertheless they obtained afterwards a grant of land from the already existing colony of Plymouth, which was in possession of a Royal Charter, and in this way they established themselves in New England. From these Puritans the population of New England is almost exclusively descended.

The zeal displayed by the colonists of Virginia in support of the royal cause during the civil war in England formed a strong contrast to the behaviour of the New England colonies. The presence of the cavaliers in Virginia contributed to strengthen the loyalty of the colonists there towards the Crown. And they remained so unshaken in their fidelity to the son of Charles I., whom they acknowledged as their king during the vicissitudes of his misfortune, that a force had to be sent out from England to reduce them to submission. On the other hand, the Puritans had espoused the cause of Cromwell with warmth from the beginning, finding a double incentive thereto in their hatred of the cavaliers and of the Established Church. It was in this way that the same dissensions, which long before had exercised their baneful influence in the Old World, came to be propagated in the New. In America a new sphere of action was thus presented for these enmities. The Puritans, who, by reason of the distance which separated them from

England, had nothing to fear, were enabled to display more energy in the promulgation of their doctrines, whereas the cavaliers, deserted by the English Government, were compelled to advocate their conservative tendency unsupported.

It is remarkable that the Puritans, who had fled from religious persecutions, soon became in America the most cruel persecutors of religious freedom and the most relentless bigots, whilst the Catholics, who had come with Lord Baltimore to Maryland under the same circumstances, were the first upon the American continent to distinguish themselves by the most decided tolerance of all religious creeds. 'While the recollection of former persecutions induced the Catholics in Maryland, the Baptists in Rhode Island, and the Quakers in Pennsylvania, to grant freedom of conscience to others, in Massachusetts, under similar circumstances, fanaticism overpowered the sense of justice.'* The same historian who relates this, describes the Puritans most admirably as follows:— 'But in truth fellow-feeling for the suffering from persecution could avail little against the fanatical bigotry of the Puritans, which infatuation, confounding all moral distinctions, regards the most savage cruelty as innocent, and converts lenity and moderation into crime.'†

Fanaticism in New England did not restrict itself

* Tucker, vol. i. p. 34.   † Ibid.

to the persecution of Dissenters. A frequent occasion for persecution was presented by the delusion of witchcraft,* the first criminal prosecutions for which took place in 1645, in Massachusetts, where four persons were executed on this charge.† Nearly half a century later, in the year 1690, this delusion had only reached its culmination.‡ These facts, taken from history, are cited to show the character and tendency of Puritanism in America. But nothing more characteristic of the spirit of that puritanical fanaticism can be found than the 'blue laws,' whose home was New England. One of these declared it to be a *crime* for a mother to kiss her babe on a Sunday.

Although these laws are no longer in force in New England, still the spirit which produced them is at present more rabid than at any previous time. And more than ever are the hothouses and sanctuaries of deluded fanaticism to be found at the firesides of New England homes. The immoral and repulsive doctrines of *Free Love*, *Spirit-rapping*, and *Woman's Rights*, owe to Christian New England their ' divine ' origin.

This puritanical fanaticism has in the present time

---

* Grahame, Colonial History, vol. iii.

† Hildreth, History of the United States of America, vol. ii. pp. 145–167.

‡ Tucker, vol. i. p. 36.

selected as the most fruitful sphere of its zealous activity the province of politics.

A natural consequence of this religious and political fanaticism is the inextinguishable hatred between the descendants of the Puritans, the people of New England, and those of the cavaliers in the South, which now appears to have reached its zenith.

This antagonism is not limited to the people of the two sections, North and South, as entire communities, but extends to the individuals of each section ; for the influence of different origin, the essentially different social and political institutions, and the diversity of education, have rendered individual character in New England and that in the Southern States irreconcilably opposite.

No one at all familiar with the state of affairs in America can fail to be impressed by the deeply-rooted hate of New Englanders towards the Southerners, whether or not it is to be attributed to the origin, refinement, or accomplishments of the latter.   And, whereas the former are accustomed to regard the Southerners with undisguised pride, these evince always an unlimited contempt for them, on account of their sordid worship of the dollar; it is, therefore, not strange that the appellation of *Yankee* should be considered in the South as synonymous with whatever is selfish and little.

Between these two people the antipathy is so great

that there appears to be no possibility of ever eradicating it. The developements of this war have made it more appreciable than ever, showing that these two people have nothing in common but the language, that they are not adapted to each other, and that therefore they cannot continue to live united in peace any longer.

Not enough importance has ever been attached to this fact, which has been one of the most potent influences that have caused the Union to be impossible.

II. *Economic Causes.*

Foreign commerce has ever been a fruitful source of bitter dissension and jealousy between the North and the South. Even before the adoption of the 'Articles of Confederation,' as well as before, and at the time of the ratification of the 'Constitution,' unmistakeable evidences of future troubles on this account among the States of both sections became manifest. In this quarter may be discovered one of the causes of the repeated acts of injustice on the part of the North towards the South.

It is well known that the North was physically more favoured in natural harbours, and consequently its people devoted themselves to commerce on the seas. And finding this a source of great wealth, the

North has employed every means at its disposal to encourage its shipping interest. Endeavouring to obtain special facilities for this purpose, the North has been utterly regardless of the interests of the other States, seeking only its own aggrandisement. Hence we find that in the making of all treaties of commerce, in the framing of navigation laws, in the introduction of tonnage duties, and particularly in arranging the regulations for the fisheries, the North has never failed to secure its purpose, often to the decided disadvantage or even injury of the South. Indeed it is notorious that on several occasions the North has been upon the point of involving the whole country in a war with England, solely in its fishing interest. With every facility at its disposal and every advantage on its side, the North also soon came to be the factors and carriers of the South, and all the coasting trade, being in its own hands, was carried on in its own ships.

On the other hand the South, not so well situated for becoming a maritime country, particularly on account of the want of such excellent harbours, found it advantageous not to become a shipping community, but rather to devote its energies to the cultivation of the soil. The North, not possessing such a productive soil as the South, turned its attention also to industrial pursuits. And so the North has finally attained such a point of excellence in them, that it is

now only second to England in the manufacture of
cotton, whilst its iron manufactures have become
very considerable.   An impetus having been given
to manufactures in the North by the war of 1812
with England, afterwards protection was sought for
the interests which had thus become engaged in
them.   Still, the plea put forward was the necessity
of a revenue for carrying on the government.   True
to this policy the North, particularly New England,
has ever since exerted itself to make the Federal
debt as heavy as possible, in order to increase the
duties on imports; for it had been found that the
duties already imposed were far more than sufficient
to defray the expenses of the government.   Now
with the immense difference in capital, population,
and ships, in favour of Europe, it is evident that the
infant manufactures of New England never could
have succeeded, had it been necessary to compete
with the old world in the home markets.   Consequently a moderate protection was at first asked and
granted; but with this assistance from the Federal
Government, the demands of the North became more
exorbitant, till finally the South openly resisted
these encroachments.   The history of the legislation
of Congress in favour of protection shows a series
of acts, each more unreasonable than the former,
tending to exclude the non-manufacturing States of
the Union from all direct trade with Europe.

Naturally the South, being the producer of only the raw material, wished to exchange its productions for manufactures in whatever markets afforded the greatest advantages. It is also obvious that Europe offered more advantages, for reasons already stated, than the North. In consequence of the protection given to Northern manufactures, competition with Europe was finally almost abolished, and by this means the North enabled to grow rich at the expense of the South. The South became the *forced customer* of the North, and the Southerner was compelled to let his money flow into the pockets of the Northerner, who in return furnished commodities of a quality inferior to those which might have been obtained at a vastly lower price, had the Southerner been at liberty to import them from Europe. In this way the trade of the South has built up the wealth of the North, enriched its cities, and given employment to its poor classes. For the results of protection were not favourable to the States as a whole, nor to the general government. The advantages resulting from it accrued solely to the population of the North. It has been estimated that the amount of indirect taxation to which the South has submitted for the last few years has reached 20,000,000*l.* annually. This estimation does not appear to be exaggerated. Thus has the South been compelled to pay tribute to the North, to enable the Northern manufacturer to compete with the European in its own markets.

If it is true that the South, while it remained in the
Union, had always been a source of wealth for the
North, it will follow that the secession of the South
from the Union must have an important effect upon
the prosperity of the North. No further proof is
needed to establish this proposition, as we have
already shown the value of the South to the North
before the separation. It is, however, worthy of
mention, that the statements made in New York to
the effect that the prosperity of the North has increased since the commencement of the war, are
devoid of all foundation in truth. For the fact that
foreign imports have decreased, whilst the exports of
the North have increased, proves the contrary. This
results from the circumstance that, in consequence of
the secession of the South, the North has ceased to
supply the South both with its own and foreign commodities. Naturally, then, the imports must have decreased, whilst the tendency of the exports was to increase, for the North found it necessary to send *abroad*
what it formerly sent to the South, whether or not with
less advantageous results we do not propose to discuss.

Such attempts on the part of Northern men to
employ weak evidence in support of their assertions,
when the contrary is manifest, as well as the loud
and passionate denunciations of the so-called treason
of the Southern States, tend to produce the thorough
conviction that the North rightly fears the most

E

fatal results from a permanent separation from the South.

Everyone is aware, however, that the tariff is a question which has been limited neither to the past nor to the present, but that from the commencement of the existence of the Union down to the moment of its dissolution, it has been a constant cause of strife. As long ago as 1832, when South Carolina proclaimed the tariff laws unconstitutional, this subject had already obtained an importance that could not be concealed. But for the last thirty years, the bitterness engendered by this cause has been increasing in intensity, till at last the South could bear no longer the injustice of this system of exorbitant protection, which amounted almost to prohibition. In the 'platform' of the 'Republican' party, which elected Mr. Lincoln, the continuance of the policy of protection was announced to be desirable and indispensable; whereas the 'Democratic' party, which had always respected the rights of the South, characterized this policy as both unwise and pernicious. The 'Republicans' have remained true to their political creed, and have placed evidence of it on record in the notorious Morrill tariff-bill, that few in Europe would be inclined to question. Here was the culmination of the efforts of the North for the last half century, against which the South had never ceased to protest and remonstrate, but with more energy and earnestness during the last thirty years.

From this system of protection has resulted an indirect taxation, which presses exclusively on the South. This the South considers, and has always considered, unconstitutional; for such it is declared to be by the provisions of the constitution [clause 1 of the seventh section of Art. I.]. This reads as follows: —

'The Congress shall have power to lay and collect taxes, duties, imposts, and excises, *to pay the debts and provide for the common defence and general welfare of the United States*; but all duties, imposts, and excises shall be *uniform* throughout the United States.'

Does not the conclusion seem inevitable on examining the purposes for which Congress can impose duties, that it has no right whatever to impose them for the aggrandisement of any one section of the Union? If it is not in order 'to pay debts and provide for the common defence and general welfare,' Congress has no power to impose any duties whatever. How much less has it, then, the right to do so *only* for the advantage of a single section. Moreover, these duties must be 'uniform throughout the United States.' When, therefore, Congress lays taxes or duties that *weigh* almost exclusively upon the South, it does what it has no constitutional right to do, and such act is unconstitutional.

Who will say, then, that the right is not here again

all on the side of the South? At least the Southerners are convinced of it, and have decided to submit
to this spoliation no more. The worst that can be
said is, that the Southern States have acted towards
the encroachments of the Union, as the thirteen
original States did towards England, when they
declared that *no taxes could lawfully be imposed upon
them without their consent.*

Because the North has tried to force these facts
into the background, let not Europe be deceived.
This was the great and chief cause of the secession
of the South; and now Europe may judge whether
this grievance was well-founded.

III. *Political Causes.*

If, in comparison with Europe, America may be
said to possess no history, still a period of time has
already elapsed sufficient for the developement of
certain political maxims in the New World, which
have been transmitted to the present generation of its
inhabitants with all the sanctity and veneration
attaching to the traditionary past. These political
principles have a double importance for them, because
they constitute the foundation upon which their
dearest rights are based. By a vindication of them

these rights were first secured. Among all of these political maxims, none is more cherished than that one announced in the 'Declaration of Independence,' and which proclaims 'that whenever any form of government becomes destructive of these ends (security of life, liberty, and the pursuit of happiness), it is the right of the people to alter or to abolish it, and to institute a new government, laying its foundation on such principles, and organizing its powers in such form, as to them shall seem most likely to effect their safety and happiness.'

The natural consequence of this principle, which obtained a real validity through the combined efforts of the thirteen original colonies, was to develope the notion of State rights; and upon this fundamental idea rested, as we have seen, the entire structure of the Union. After so many sacrifices had been made, and so much suffering endured to establish the sovereignty of the individual States, it is self-evident that every attempt on the part of the Federal Government to violate this principle must have been regarded by the States as an injury not to be submitted to.

At an early period commenced a series of acts on the part of the general government, which have resulted in rendering the Union impossible. At one time we find the Federal Government asserting its exclusive jurisdiction over the Indian lands situated within the limits of certain States. This produced, very naturally, a feeling of resentment on the part of the States interested, which were Southern States, so that on several occasions resort was about being made to arms to defend their rights.

For a long time the South has been aggrieved by the action of Congress respecting the district of Columbia. It is well known that this district was acquired from the States of Maryland and Virginia for the seat of the Federal Government, under the express conditions that no law should be made by Congress for the government of the district which might be hostile to the institutions of the above-named States; unless, at least, these States should give their express consent to the same. The Federal Congress has continually exerted itself to escape the fulfilment of these conditions. Efforts have constantly been made to abolish slavery in the district by direct legislation of Congress, regardless of the self-imposed condition not to interfere with it at all. We say that Congress has tried to effect this result, for in point of fact there never was a sufficient majority in Congress to accomplish it, until the separation of the South. But the recurring threats and attempts to effect it had served to irritate the South greatly, and to convince the Southern people that when the party in the North hostile to their institutions should obtain the supremacy in Congress, the Federal

Government would not hesitate a moment to legislate slavery out of the district, and then, going a step further, would combat slavery and attempt its overthrow in the Southern States themselves. Yet everybody knows that Congress has no right to interfere with the internal affairs of any State, least of all about slavery, which was recognised by the constitution: for this is not among the powers delegated to Congress.

When Missouri sought admission into the Union in 1820, having the requisite population, it was at first refused by the Northern vote. At last the admission was only allowed under the condition, that for the future slavery should not exist in any territory north of 36° 30'. This was a flagrant violation of the constitution, which does not give to Congress the right to refuse admission to any territory having the required population, provided the constitution of such territory be Republican. 'On that event,' says Rawle,* ' the inhabitants acquire a right to assemble and form a constitution for themselves, and the United States are considered as bound to admit the new State into the Union, provided its form of government be that of a representative Republic. This is, perhaps, the only check or control possessed by the United States.'

At the time that Congress passed this unconsti-

* William Rawle, l. c. p. 294.

tutional act, the Southern States protested by their
votes against the measure, and proclaimed it to be
unconstitutional.

The constant efforts that had been made to exclude
the South from the Territories, which are the common
property of all the States alike, aroused the indignation of the Southern people most thoroughly.   It
will not be pretended that the rights of one State in
the Territories were greater than those of another.
The citizens of the Northern States were at liberty
to take their property with them into the Territories
and were protected in their possession of it.   Why
was it, then, that when the citizens of the Southern
States, emigrating thither with their property in
slaves, which were recognised as such by the constitution, claimed the same protection for their species
of property, as that accorded to other kinds of
personal property in the Territories, legal protection
was denied by the Federal Government?   Plainly it
was an act of injustice and usurpation in favour of
the North, and an attempt to exclude the South
from all participation in the Territories.   A confirmation of this is to be seen in the legislation of
Congress with respect to the public lands in the
Territories.   The lands were squandered, or sold at
pitiably low prices, in order to attract the poor
classes of the North, and to direct the emigration
thither from Europe, it being known that the South

could spare comparatively few of its citizens for populating the new Territories. With what success this has been carried out, let the election of Mr. Lincoln by the foreign vote attest.

The interference of Congress with slavery was the more uncalled-for, seeing that a territory, once admitted, would have an unquestionable right to establish slavery, or to abolish it, by changing its constitution accordingly. There is nothing in the constitution that prevents any Northern State from introducing slavery within its limits, if it should choose to do so. If Massachusetts should to-morrow discover African slavery to be the most profitable kind of labour for its manufactures, and if the people should accordingly decide upon introducing it into that State, there is no power in the constitution of the United States which can prevent it. On the other hand, there is no power in the same instrument which can prevent any State from abolishing slavery at will.

As members of the Federal pact, it was incumbent upon the States to act always, and strictly in good faith towards each other in executing the provisions of the constitution. A sense of honour alone should have compelled them to do so. Has this been the way in which the North has acted towards the South? Let their ' Personal Liberty bills ' be the answer. Judge Story, the eminent jurist, and celebrated opponent of slavery, has stated that the Union never could have been framed without the mutual obligation of the rendition of fugitive slaves, as provided for by the constitution. It was indeed a most wanton violation of the constitution to attempt to evade the performance of duties enjoined by it. But when we consider that the rendition of fugitive slaves was made obligatory upon the Northern States by their own free assent to the constitution, the unceasing efforts made for a series of years to endanger the rights of the South, by evading this obligation, appear doubly wicked. The rendition of fugitive slaves was one of the fundamental rights of the South, but in a large number of the Northern States 'Personal Liberty bills' were passed, which, making it punishable by fine and imprisonment for citizens of these States to assist in the capture of any fugitive, rendered the execution of the constitution impossible. It is no reply to this that, according to the census of 1850, one slave escaped to each 2,527 held in bondage in the border Slave States; whereas, according to that of 1860, one escaped only to each 3,276. In a population of 1,638,297 slaves in these border States, this is an average loss of 500 slaves, or a loss of 100,000*l.* annually.

To these political causes may be added those belonging properly to the sphere of religion.

Americans are accustomed to regard religion and everything pertaining thereto as one of the most im-

portant and serious affairs of life. Until within a
few years past, religious societies had managed to keep
aloof from the arena of politics. The Methodists
were the first denomination that incorporated the
question of slavery in their religious creed, and thereby created two parties. Afterwards the Baptists,
and then the Presbyterians, followed their example.
Thus was a division made in religion, which, taking
a deep hold on the passions of men, was productive
of the most deplorable results. The opponents of
slavery characterized the system as the chief sin of
the human race, and declared it unpardonable to remain in the same religious union with those enter-
taining other views. In fact, when we consider the
full extent and significance of this event, we are led
to conclude that, with the dissolution of the religious
union on the question of slavery, all hopes for the
preservation of the political union were dissipated.

Another powerful lever for the dissolution of the
Union was the abuse of the sacred desk. The clergy
of the North did not consider it inconsistent with
their sacred calling to declare their political senti-
ments from the pulpit, and that in the most fanatical
way.

The constitution which recognised slavery was
denounced as 'a league with death, and a covenant
with hell,' and in this way the right asserted to
disregard the constitution in its relations to slavery.

Such impious doctrines met with greater approval, because the piously inclined hearers were disposed to receive as truth the maxims pronounced by their clergy, with less criticism and examination, than if they had been uttered by other teachers; and so, the wish of fanatical priests was confounded with the word of God.

But on the growing youth such fanatical doctrines exerted a more lasting influence, because the thus educated representatives of the people and future members of Congress, imbibing those heresies with their mothers' milk, and rearing upon that sandy foundation the edifice of their political faith, became accustomed to consider the violation of the constitution as justifiable by the 'higher law.'

Also, the vehement abuse that has only too often been uttered and written against the South, contributed not a little to widening the breach. Without any foundation it has been asserted repeatedly that the South violated the laws in regard to the slave-trade; but it is known that all the slave-ships fitted out in America for the slave-trade between Africa and the West Indies are Northern ships, with Northern or foreign crews, which are sent out by Northern capitalists, while the odium of breaking the treaties for the suppression of this traffic is cast upon the South. Moreover, this does not stand to reason when we bear in mind that most all of the Southern

States have laws still in force, and in many cases ante-
rior in date to the constitution, which forbid the importation of African slaves from Africa into their borders.

With equal injustice has the North contended that
the notorious arrogance and insolence, which have
characterized the political intercourse of the United
States Government with foreign nations, were to be
attributed to the South. The only argument advanced to support this assumption was the fact that
the former Presidents were chiefly those chosen by
the South; whereas, in 'the nineteen presidential
elections, sixteen of those that have been elected have
received more electoral votes in the North than in
the South. *Sixteen have also received a majority of
the electoral votes of the Northern States*, while *only
three* were chosen in opposition to the North by
Southern States, in combination with a powerful
Northern majority.'* For the future at least the
South desires to see her interests represented in
Europe with that courtesy which is usual in other
countries, except in the North of America.

Here belong, furthermore, the calumnies propagated
against the South by the North. Among these was
the charge that the South encouraged filibustering
expeditions against Cuba, which, it was contended,
lying near to the South, and having the institution of

* Williams. The South Vindicated, London, 1862, p. 337. Some interesting comparisons of the presidential elections are to be found here.

African slavery, the South was anxious to annex. The indefensibility of this reasoning shows itself at the first glance at the fact, that the acquisition of Cuba by the United States would have been diametrically opposed to the interests of the South; for this island would, in that event, have satisfied its demand for labour, for slaves, by drawing its supply from the Southern States, as in that case the laws against the slave-trade would prevent their further introduction from Africa. But the South has not enough of this kind of labour for itself, and therefore the loss of its slaves by exportation to Cuba could not fail to be most serious in its consequences to the Southern States.

Emigration from Europe also has contributed its full share to the dissolution of the Union. The greater part of these emigrants, particularly since the year 1848, consisted of political malcontents, persons without property, often fugitives from justice, fanatical and embittered spirits, who brought with them those socialistic ideas, only too much in consonance with the red Republican doctrines of the Radicals in the North. These persons pretended to see in the prosperous slave-holding Southerners their hereditary enemies, and therefore, looking at the question of slavery from a purely ideal standpoint, helped to fan into full flame the slumbering fires of discord, using the dissensions of the two sections with a real fanaticism for their own selfish ends, after receiving homes almost without cost at the hands of the Federal Government.

Finally, it may be added that the impression disseminated by the North, that the election of Mr. Lincoln was the sole cause of the dissolution of the Union, is absolutely false. This was the result of consummate malice on the part of the North, in order to place the Southerners in a false light before Europe, as rebels. We say this was done maliciously, for never has it occurred to the South to dispute the constitutionality of Lincoln's election, at least as far as the form of it is concerned. It is consequently false when the North asserts that the South, spoiled by the elections of its former presidential candidates in combination with the Democratic party of the North, could not bear the galling idea of submitting to be governed by a man who belonged to another political party. No; it was not the unconstitutionality of Lincoln's election, who, it is true, while receiving the majority of votes in the Electoral College, only received 1,857,610 of the 4,715,270 electoral votes cast, but other reasons, which caused secession. It was the well-founded apprehension that the advocates of the principles of the 'Republican' party, a party undisguisedly hostile to the South, would soon gain the supremacy in Congress, and, in cooperation with their political ally, the new President, would proceed to trample under foot the rights of the Southern

States; it was the apprehension that this party, passing soon from words to deeds, would attempt to execute their unconstitutional intentions with respect to slavery, when it would have been too late to think about withdrawing from the Union. Secession had long been viewed in the South as the last means at command to prevent the destruction of constitutional liberty and justice in America. And now, when Lincoln was elected, the South realized that the long anticipated time had arrived, and that it was necessary to *act* before its independence and liberty were for ever lost.

But indeed, what importance was to be attached to the election of Mr. Lincoln? Lincoln was the victorious candidate of a purely sectional party. Nothing similar to this had ever before occurred. A President elected against the unanimous protest of every State in the South, and elected solely by the votes of its declared enemies. This was not the cause of secession, but only the occasion of it.

Had the necessary guarantees asked for by the South always been accorded, and had the North always given sufficient grounds for confidence in the conscientious observation of the constitution, as very rightly demanded by the South, the Southern States would have acquiesced in the election of Lincoln, and there would have been no cause for secession. Had the North been less abusive in its relations with the South, it is not impossible that for a number of years to come the South would have remained passive, and suffered itself to be plundered, as had already been the case for a long time.

Can any unprejudiced mind now doubt that the time had come when the South, standing *alone*, without any guarantees for the observation of the constitution, was obliged to act? On the contrary, an examination of the numerous social, economic, and political causes already recorded, all contributing in a greater or less degree, perhaps unequally, to jeopardise the existence of the Union, must establish the conviction that the moment had really arrived, when the liberty, the rights, the welfare, and the honour of the South must compel it to dissolve those now only external bonds, which united it to a Union that had long since ceased to exist in the spirit of the constitution.

CHAPTER III.

THE WAR.

I. *Unconstitutionality of the War.*

By the constitution it is expressly provided that *Congress alone* shall have the right to *declare war* and *to raise and support armies.* The power is also given to *Congress* 'to provide for calling forth the militia to execute the laws of the Union, suppress insurrections, and rebel invasions.'* We have already cited the authority of Rawle,† to show that it is only in the event that a faction should attempt to subvert the government of a State that 'the case provided for (by this clause of the constitution) will have arisen, and the Union is bound to employ its power to prevent it.' It has been attempted to prove that the withdrawal of a State, secession, from the Union is not only *the legitimate exercise of State sovereignty,* but also a *constitutional right*; it is therefore neither opposition to the laws of the Union nor

---

* Constitution. Art. I. Sect. 8.
† William Rawle, l. c. p. 292.

rebellion. Hence it follows, that not even *Congress* itself, least of all the *President*, had the right to oppose to the secession of the Southern States *armed force*. We direct attention here to the fact, that in the debates of the Convention at Philadelphia in 1787 Madison observed:

'The use of force against a State would look more like a declaration of war than an infliction of punishment; and would probably be considered by the party attacked as a dissolution of all previous compacts by which it might be bound. He hoped that such a system would be framed as might render this resource unnecessary, and moved that the clause be postponed.' This motion was agreed to *unanimously*.* And never since that time has there been a question of coercion.

In recent times, also, has this principle been confirmed. Even President Buchanan has supported it. He says :†

'The question fairly stated is — Has the constitution delegated to Congress the power to coerce a State into submission which is attempting to withdraw, or has actually withdrawn, from the confederacy? If answered in the affirmative, it must be on the principle that the power has been conferred upon Congress to declare and make war against a State.

* Madison Papers, vol. ii. p. 761.
† President Buchanan's Message to Congress, December 3, 1860.

After much serious reflection, I have arrived at the conclusion that no such power has been delegated to Congress or to any other department of the Federal Government. It is manifest, upon an inspection of the constitution, that this is not among the specific and enumerated powers granted to Congress; and it is equally apparent that its exercise is not " necessary and proper for carrying into execution" any one of these powers. So far from this power having been delegated to Congress, it was expressly refused by the convention which framed the constitution.

' Without descending to particulars it may be safely asserted, that the power to make war against a State is at variance with the whole spirit and intent of the constitution. Suppose such a war should result in the conquest of a State, how are we to govern it afterwards? Shall we hold it as a province, and govern it by despotic force ? In the nature of things we could not, by physical force, control the will of the people, and compel them to elect senators and re-presentatives to Congress, and to perform all the other duties depending on their own volition, and required from the free citizens of a free State as a constituent member of the confederacy.

' But if we possessed the power, would it be wise to exercise it under the circumstances? The object would, doubtless, be to preserve the Union. War would not only present the most effectual means of destroying it, but would banish all hope of its peaceable reconstruction. Besides, in the fraternal conflict a vast amount of blood and treasure would be expended, rendering future reconstruction between the States impossible. In the meantime, who can foretell what would be the sufferings and privations of the people during its existence?

'The fact is that our Union rests upon public opinion, and can never be cemented by the blood of its citizens shed in civil war. If it cannot live in the affections of the people, it must one day perish. Congress possesses many means of preserving it by conciliation; but the sword was not placed in their hands to preserve it by force.'

II. *Commencement of the War.*

The secession of the State of South Carolina in 1860 had been regarded beforehand as a possible event; nevertheless, public opinion in the North was not sufficiently prepared to realize all the significance attaching to it. On several previous occasions the Southern States had threatened to resume the exercise of their delegated authority, and consequently the North, particularly New England, was disposed to consider this last threat another bugbear.

When the Convention of South Carolina passed the ordinance of secession, commissioners were despatched

to the Federal Government to commence negotiations
respecting the claims of both parties, and to agree
upon the terms of their adjustment. At the same
time a demand was made upon the Federal Government to withdraw its troops from the forts in the
harbour of Charleston. It is true that these forts
were Federal property, which had been acquired with
the consent of South Carolina; this was not disputed,
but South Carolina demanded that the Federal
Government should evacuate them, pledging itself, in
the settlement of their mutual claims, to grant full
indemnity for the outlay that had been 'made in
constructing the forts. Now that South Carolina
had determined to undertake the protection of its
own coast, the Federal Government could no longer
pretend to any right to retain the forts; for it was
self-evident that South Carolina could not submit to
the presence of foreign troops on its soil. President
Buchanan, however, refused to recognise these commissioners as the representatives of a foreign State,
and declined to accede to their demand.

Nevertheless, the commissioners remained in
Washington, seeking to accomplish their purpose by
obtaining an acknowledgement of their claims; they
limited their demands, however, for the moment to
the extent, that no reinforcements whatever should
be sent to Fort Sumter. On the other hand, they
agreed to permit the small garrison to remain in the

forts, South Carolina binding itself not to attack them, so long as the stipulation not to send reinforcements should be observed by the Federal Government. President Buchanan acceded to this proposal, and communicated the result to Congress in his message of January 8, 1861. At the same time he attempted to justify the promise made to the commissioners, by the desire to avoid the commencement of hostilities; as South Carolina had given assurance of its intention to regard any attempt to send reinforcements to Charleston, or to change the status quo of the forts, as a declaration of war on the part of the United States. The President desired the more to avoid a bloody collision, as he still cherished the hope of restoring the Union by moderation.

When Mr. Lincoln was inaugurated as Mr. Buchanan's successor, and took an oath before assembled Congress to observe the constitution, he, too, refused to acknowledge the commissioners from South Carolina as the representatives of an independent State; still he caused Mr. Seward to enter into a correspondence with them, in which the engagement entered into by Mr. Buchanan was not repudiated, consequently silently acknowledged.

Mr. Seward favoured a peaceful adjustment of the difficulty; and his influence, it is said, caused Mr. Lincoln also to desire a peaceful solution in the beginning. We are indebted to Governor Pickens of South Carolina, however, for information respecting the motives which induced President Lincoln, at the expiration of a few weeks, suddenly to reverse his policy. Soon after the commencement of hostilities, Governor Pickens caused the history of the negotiations at Washington to be published over his own name in one of the journals of the State.* We insert this document, as tending to throw a great deal of light upon the secret history of the war.

'State of South Carolina.
'Head-quarters: Aug. 3, 1861.

'I have every reason, from information received by me in the most confidential manner (not forbidding publication, however), and through one very near the most intimate counsels of the President of the United States, to induce me to believe that the following article was submitted, as a proof sheet, to Mr. Lincoln and his Cabinet; that a proclamation, in conformity with its general views, was to be issued; and that a change in the decision of the Cabinet was made in one night, when exactly the contrary course was adopted. It is asserted in this article (which in all probability is a proof sheet from a confidential New York paper), that if the President desired to excite and madden the whole North to a war of

* The Columbia 'South Carolinian' of August 3, 1861.

extermination against slavery, and in favour of the absolute plunder and conquest of the South, he had only to resolve that Major Anderson and his garrison and Fort Sumter should perish, as it appears was well known would have to be the case. Major Anderson and his men were to be used as fuel, to be thrown in to kindle the flames of fanaticism, and to force the Northern people into a united war, which would give the Abolition leaders absolute control over the Government and country. What must be the feelings of the civilised world when it is known that the President of the United States and his Cabinet did so act, and with a view expressly to carry out this policy of exciting the whole Northern mind?

'Major Anderson had officially informed the former Administration that he could hold Fort Sumter; and, of course, if the object of that Administration was to betray the Government into the hands of the Secessionists, as is charged in the article, then Major Anderson must have been a party to the treason; and if he informed the new President, on the 4th of March, as is said to be the case, that he could not hold the fort, then he acted out his part fully in aiding to place Mr. Lincoln and his Cabinet exactly where they were, and to compel them to evacuate the fortress, or to use the garrison as victims, to be slaughtered on the unholy altar of blind fanaticism and mad ambition.

' I know the fact from Mr. Lincoln's most intimate
friend and accredited agent, Mr. Lamon, that the
President of the United States professed a desire to
evacuate Fort Sumter, and he (Mr. Lamon) actually
wrote me, after his return to Washington, that he
would be back in a few days to aid in that purpose.
Major Anderson was induced to expect the same
thing, as his notes to me prove. I know the fact
that Mr. Fox, of the United States Navy, after obtaining permission from me, upon the express gua-
rantee of a former gallant associate in the navy, to
visit Major Anderson " for pacific purposes," planned
the pretended attempts to relieve and reinforce the
garrison by a fleet, and that Major Anderson protested against it. I now believe that it was all a
scheme, and that Fox's disgraceful expedition was
gotten up in concert with Mr. Lincoln, merely to
delude the Northern public into the belief that they
intended to sustain and protect Major Anderson,
when, in fact, according to the article now published
for the first time, they decided to do no such thing,
and acted with the deliberate intention to let the
garrison perish, that they might thereby excite the
North, and rouse them to unite in this unholy and
unnatural war, by which the desperate and profligate
leaders of an infuriated and lawless party might
gratify their vengeance and lust of power over the

ruins of their country, and amid the blind passions of a maddened people.

'The document now published, and the peculiar circumstances, show the basest and most infamous motives that have ever actuated the rulers of any people, except, perhaps, in the days of the first French revolution, when history shows that wholesale murder was often planned by insurrectionists in Paris, under the deliberate guidance of malignant leaders, whose whole objects were universal plunder and murder, in order to exterminate one party and ride into power themselves.

'A moment's review of the line of argument pursued in the article, will show that the policy finally adopted in regard to Fort Sumter was intended and desired by Mr. Lincoln and his advisers to lead to a war, not to be regulated by the rules and usages among civilized people, but to one of rapine, murder, and utter extermination of the people against whom it was intended to be waged, founded upon no principle of right, seeking not to reestablish any disputed authority, or establish any other object than to gratify a lust for power and revenge.

'For the purpose of directly proving the motives and impulses of the United States Government in the inauguration of this war, it is only necessary to make several extracts from the article in question, as they will serve also to direct the special attention of the public to those portions which most vividly prove the unhallowed purposes of President Lincoln and his advisers.

' One of the chief ends of the article seems to have been the proof of treason on the part of President Buchanan, and through all of it runs the oft-repeated "alternative" left them by him of "permitting Major Anderson and his command to starve within fifteen days," or of ignominiously abandoning it to a nest of "unprincipled rebels."

*   *   *   *   *

' It was intended to show that the object of President Lincoln was to preserve "peace," not to "make war;" to "protect the sacred Constitution" confided to his keeping, and to gain over, by his avowedly peaceful objects, those who had defied that "Constitution" and broken its laws. It is asserted that President Lincoln could not suppress the "tears" of anguish which his signing the order for the evacuation of Fort Sumter called forth, and it is said, too, that he desired to "discharge his duty to humanity;" and yet he has chosen to "discharge" that "duty" in the singular way of resolving on a policy which, in his own words, he knew would "raise throughout the mighty North a feeling of indignation, which in ninety days would have emancipated every slave on the continent, and driven their masters into the sea."

'The sacrifice was made; Anderson and his command were forced to become liable as victims to fanaticism; Fort Sumter was wrapt in flames; and yet, forsooth, they tell us that the only man who could have prevented it was "resolved to discharge his duty to humanity," and that his purpose was " peace "— his aversion " war." His "purpose " was changed, and he resolved to bring on this unhallowed war. It is a Government actuated with *these* feelings that we are to defend ourselves against; it is *this* kind of war, then, that the people of the South are to meet; and under these circumstances it becomes my duty to publish the article in question for the information of the people of the Confederate States, and for the cool and unbiassed contemplation of the civilised world.

'A war thus inaugurated — from such motives and under such circumstances — surely can never meet with the favour of heaven. A people educated and trained up to constitutional liberty can never, for any length of time, sustain such a war.

'F. W. PICKENS.'

ABANDONMENT OF FORT SUMTER.

NECESSITY KNOWS NO LAW.

There are periods in the history of nations and individuals, when the force of even this proverb is illustrated. The law, or rather the demands of justice, self-respect, national honour, and the vindication of our nationality in the eyes of Europe, all demand that we should retain possession of Fort Sumter at any and every sacrifice; and no man in this nation is more deeply impressed with the paramount importance of so doing, than is Abraham Lincoln, the President of the United States. He feels and recognises his duty in the premises; but the law of necessity steps in, puts at defiance his wishes and his duty, and sternly forbids his attempting to hold or relieve the noble fortress so promptly snatched from the hands of the rebels and traitors of Charleston, by the timely action of Major Anderson. Buchanan and his traitor Cabinet had deliberately planned the robbing of our arsenals, under the superintendence, and with the connivance of the miserable fellow Floyd, whose portrait now hangs so conspicuously in the Rogue's Gallery of our City Police; and we all know, that when Major Anderson took possession of Fort Sumter, Floyd demanded its restoration to the rebels, and that Buchanan actually yielded to the demand, until threatened with danger to his person if he ventured upon any such act of treachery. He yielded to a stern necessity; but in yielding he determined to accomplish by management and finesse what he had not the courage to do openly. He accordingly refused to permit the fort to be reinforced, as it could have been in those days, with the necessary men and stores to enable it to hold out for a year at least against any force which could be brought against it; and it was not until after Morris's Island had been fortified, that he sanctioned the abortive attempt at succour made by the Star of the West; and even countermanded that order before it was carried into effect.

' From Christmas until March 4, the traitors and rebels of Charleston and the cotton States, received every countenance and support from Mr. Buchanan which could be afforded them; and when he retired from office on the 4th instant, he gloated over the conviction that he had fostered rebellion and treason until they had become so rampant, that they were beyond the control of his successor. And the one great source of his glorification was, that Fort Sumter was without provisions; and that of necessity, the garrison must surrender from starvation before it would be in the power of the Republican Administration to relieve and reinforce it.

' Of course, Abraham Lincoln could know nothing of this treason; and when in his inaugural he spoke of occupying the public forts and collecting the revenue, he little dreamed that his predecessor had treasonably arranged to make the abandonment of Fort Sumter a political *necessity*. He was soon apprised, however, that the *treason* of his predecessor

had cunningly devised for him the most serious mor-
tification that could be inflicted; and that he had
presented to him the alternative of permitting
Anderson and his command to *starve* or promptly to
withdraw them, and ignominiously permit the fort
to fall into the hands of the rebels. To reinforce
the garrison or to supply them with provisions is
equally impossible, for James Buchanan, and his
associate traitors, designedly refused to do so while
it was in their power to do it; and compelled the
commandant of the fort quietly to permit the construction of works in his immediate vicinity, and
under the range of his guns, which would effectually
prevent his being relieved when an honest man
assumed the Government on March 4. Buchanan's
final act of treason has been consummated. He
prevented the last Congress from passing a law
giving power to the Executive to call for volunteers to occupy and recapture the public forts and
arsenals, and he designedly left Fort Sumter in a
position which renders relief physically impossible
without an army of from 10,000 to 20,000 men,
and the employment of a naval force greater than
we can command; and he and his myrmidons now
exultingly and tauntingly say to the Republican
President: " Do your worst. We have designedly
withheld from you the means of relieving and holding Fort Sumter, and we invite you to the pleasing

alternative of permitting Anderson and his command to *starve* within fifteen days, or of ignominiously abandoning it to a nest of traitors and rebels, whom we have nursed into existence as the only certain mode of destroying the Republican party."

'Such are the simple facts of the case as they are presented to the new President upon his assuming the reins of Government; and we speak advisedly and from knowledge, when we say that, while the country has been wickedly made to believe that the time of the Administration has been occupied with the disposal of offices, four-fifths of all the hours spent in consultation by the Cabinet have been devoted to the consideration of the all-important question — How to save Fort Sumter, and avert from the Government the dishonour of abandoning it to the miserable traitors who, for months, have been in open rebellion against the authority of the Government? Generals Scott and Totten, and all the military and naval chiefs at Washington, have been consulted; every plan which military science could conceive, or military daring suggest, has been attentively considered and maturely weighed, with a hope, at least, that the work of the traitor Buchanan was not so complete as he and his associates supposed. But all in vain. There stands the isolated naked fact—Fort Sumter cannot be relieved because of the treason of the late Administration, and

Major Anderson and his command must perish by starvation unless withdrawn.

'What, then, is to be done? Could the President leave them to starve? *Cui bono?* Would the sacrifice of a handful of gallant men to the treason of thieves and rebels have been grateful to their countrymen? But, says the indignant yet thoughtless patriot, "think of the humiliation and dishonour of abandoning Sumter to the rebels!" We do think of it, and weep tears of blood over the humiliation thus brought upon the country by the traitor President, who has just retired to Wheatland to gloat over his consummated treason. And we are assured, too, and do not doubt the truth of the assurance, that when Abraham Lincoln was compelled to yield his reluctant consent to this most humiliating concession to successful treason, he did not attempt to suppress the sorrow and tears which it called forth. But he had no alternative. "Necessity knows no law;" and to save the lives of the gallant men who have so long held Fort Sumter against an overwhelming force of heartless traitors and wicked and unprincipled rebels, whose treason has been steeped in fraud and theft, vulgarly known as "Southern chivalry," the President of the United States, in the discharge of a duty to humanity, has signed the order for the evacuation of Sumter.

'Had war, not peace, been his object — had he desired to raise throughout the mighty North a feeling of indignation, which in ninety days would have emancipated every slave on the continent and driven their masters into the sea, if needs be—he had only to have said: "Let the garrison of Fort Sumter do their duty and perish beneath its walls; and on the heads of the traitors and rebels of the slavery propagandists be the consequences." Such a decision would have carried joy to the bosoms of Phillips and Garrison and their fanatical associates, who so justly consider abolitionism and disunion synonymous; but it would have brought upon the country such scenes of horror as the mind shrinks from contemplating. Verily, the blood of the martyrs would have been the seed of "Negro emancipation." For every patriot soldier thus sacrificed to the revival of the African slave-trade and the establishment of a hideous slaveocracy at the South, ten thousand negro slaves would have been emancipated, and as many of their masters driven into the ocean to expiate their crimes on earth.

'But Mr. Lincoln desired to rouse no such feeling of revenge among the people of the free States. He knew—no man knew better—that he had but to hold on to Fort Sumter, agreeably to the plainly expressed will of the people, and leave its gallant garrison to the fate prepared for them by rebels and traitors, to insure an uprising which would at once

wipe out slavery from the face of the country, and
with it all engaged in this atrocious rebellion
against the Government. But his purpose is peace,
not war. His object is to restore, to rebuild, and to
preserve the Government and the constitution which
enacted it, and his great aim is, while maintaining
the constitution and enforcing the laws, to bring
back good men to their allegiance, and leave the
thieves, and rogues, and braggarts who compose the
great mass of the rebels, under the cognomen of
" Southern Chivalry," to the uninterrupted enjoyment of their own precious society, and the reflections
which time must awaken even in them. He is
mindful of his oath " registered in heaven," to preserve the constitution and enforce the laws; and he
feels that his mission is to reclaim, and not extin-
guish, or he would most assuredly have left Fort
Sumter to its fate, and that fate would have been
speedy, certain, and absolute annihilation to the
traitors now in rebellion against the Government,
and to the very existence of the institution of slavery
on the American continent. But he has been faithful to his oath of office and to the constitution; and
by yielding to the necessity of the case and listening
to the cry of humanity, slavery has had accorded to it
its last victory over freedom and the constitution of
the United States.

' The deed has been accomplished; the sacrifice has

been made; traitors and rebels are again triumphant; and the stars and stripes are again to be dishonoured in the sight of the nation and of astonished Europe; the flag of the Union is to be pulled down, and the bloody banner of pirates, freebooters, rebels, and traitors is to be run up to wave triumphantly over Fort Sumter, and be saluted from hundreds of guns in the rebel camp, amid the cheers of thousands whose senseless gasconade and braggadocio vauntings have long since disgusted brave men and honest citizens. And yet we approve the act. A traitor President rendered it a necessity, and humanity demanded that Abraham Lincoln should sacrifice all personal feelings, and gracefully yield to that necessity and the deliberately planned treason upon which it is based. His countrymen will sustain him in the discharge of a humiliating but an imperative duty; but, with him, they feel that the account is now closed with treason. There is nothing now to yield to traitors—nothing more to sacrifice in order to give slavery and the slave-trade the odour of nationality. In future the President of the United States has only laws to enforce and a constitution to sustain; and woe be to them who thwart him in the performance of his duty, and to himself if he dares to shrink from the performance of his whole duty.'

Conformably to the original desire of Mr. Lincoln to evacuate Fort Sumter, the commissioners had

been quieted with the assurance that no effort would
be made to relieve that garrison; but, as seen from
the foregoing, the President suddenly changed his
policy, and South Carolina, considering this as breach
of the peace, took measures for self-defence.

This unexampled want of good faith strengthened
the other Southern States in their distrust of Lincoln
and his party; it revealed to them the character of
the 'Republican' President with whom they had to
deal; and thus nothing was more natural than their
secession from the Union.

The action of Lincoln must, then, be regarded as
a purely party manœuvre, by which it was designed
to obtain permanent supremacy for his party, and
absolute control of the Government. The conception
of this plan by Lincoln was well devised; it was
foreseen that, in the immense popular excitement
sure to ensue, few persons in the North would stop
to question the constitutionality of his proceedings;
and that even those having the hardihood to do so
would be powerless to harm him, whilst the mob
sustained him in his course with its approval.

Everyone is aware of the success that attended
Lincoln's calculations; Fort Sumter was bombarded
and forced to capitulate; the cry for vengeance was
sounded throughout the length and breadth of the
land; and President Lincoln proclaimed the bom-
bardment of Fort Sumter to be treason against the

Union, while it was, in fact, only the beginning of hostilities for self-defence that had been forced upon South Carolina by an act of the Federal Government, which, it was known, would be regarded as a declaration of war.

The next important official act of the new President, who had only a few weeks previously sworn to observe the constitution, was a clear violation of his oath and of the constitution, by raising an army of 75,000 men to wage war against the liberty and rights of the South. The administration thus commenced by a reckless disregard of the solemn nature of an oath, and by a violation of the constitution, has continued to disgrace itself by a series of the most flagrant violations of it, and has served to mark President Lincoln as a man who has reduced it to the perfection of a trade, to trample under foot with despotic violence almost all the constitutional rights of the once free American people.

III. *Character of the War—on the part of the North, a means for the acquisition of greater power; on the part of the South, for securing its independence and liberty.*

The former territory of the United States consisted of two political divisions—the one comprising the thirty-four States, the other the Territories. The

latter contain but a limited population; for being
situated mostly in the interior, with little or no
direct communication with the sea, they do not offer
the same attractions for emigration as many of the
States. Of the thirty-four States, fifteen are Southern,
the so-called Slave States; these comprise an extent
of territory as great as that of the other nineteen
States, having an area of more than 800,000 square
miles—a country possessing one of the most productive soils of the world for agriculture, whilst abounding in almost inexhaustible treasures of minerals.
Thirteen of the Southern States have already formally
seceded from the Union; another, Maryland, is completely in the possession of a Northern army, and
prevented by force from joining the Confederate
States; while only Delaware, the smallest of all, has
remained in the Union.

The Mississippi river, which drains the entire North-
West, flows through the centre of the seceded States;
its mouths and a great part of its extent are commanded by these same States; and thus the products
of the North-West, in passing over this natural commercial highway, have to traverse a foreign country.
The importance of the Mississippi for the North-
West is almost incalculable, and must cause that section to cultivate the most friendly relations with the
nation possessing its mouths; for it is the only natural outlet for the varied and rich products of

this fertile country. Without it, direct communication with Europe would be cut off almost entirely; while it is at the same time the most convenient, and the cheapest route for transportation to market. The North is therefore compelled to prevent, if possible, the West, the richest part of its territory, from becoming dependent on a foreign nation for a natural outlet for its productions. It is only by retaining possession of this great river that the North-West can remain commercially independent, and the war already commenced is prosecuted with energy to secure this result.

The free population of the United States amounted in 1860 to 27,477,090 souls; that of the Southern States to 8,352,385, to which number must be added 3,952,738 slaves. Without the South the whole population of the North would amount to only 19,124,705 inhabitants; the war is therefore waged to retain this entire population, which the North hopes to control by its superiority in numbers.

The white and black populations of the South together amount to 12,305,123 souls. But the South, as we have seen, has always been the chief, and almost exclusive market for the manufactures of the North; the war is carried on therefore to retain twelve and a half millions of forced customers for the products of Northern industry. The South has also been made to contribute far more than its proportion

of the means for administering the Federal Government. This war is intended to secure not only the
control of a greater power, but along with it to
obtain, also, the chief means of its support.

Should the South succeed in achieving its independence, the North must submit to see the great
Southern trade, which formerly passed through its
cities, take new channels, and be carried on directly
between Europe and the ports of the South. With
the loss of the Southern export and import trade
would vanish the Northern monopoly of the coasting
trade; while the shipping interest generally of the
North would suffer to an almost incredible extent.
Thus would perish the very foundations upon which
the commercial and industrial prosperity of the North
rested. A successful termination of the war alone
can avert all these evils from the North.

An inevitable consequence of the triumph of the
South would be additional secessions from the Union.
First of all the North-West would, for reasons already
intimated, withdraw from the Federal league; its
interests are too intimately identified with those of
the South for it to remain connected with the North;
the protective policy of the Union will be found to
be as inimical to the prosperity of the North-West, as
it was oppressive to the South; and self-interest will
prompt this great section to leave the North and
join its fortunes with those of the South, or else,

constituting itself into an independent State, to form
an alliance of friendship with the States having
control of the Mississippi.   Nor must it be forgotten
that the North-West will, most probably, refuse to
pay any part of the enormous debt incurred for the
prosecution of a war, the unconstitutionality of which
will become evident to it with time.

On the Pacific Ocean as well, will the States there
situated form themselves into a confederacy; for Cali-
fornia, Oregon, and the Territories of the far West,
being already geographically separated from the rest
by the Rocky Mountains, will naturally find it to
their interest to form a league among themselves.
Indeed, we might venture to predict that within a
not very remote period of time, all the States will
have withdrawn from New England, the original and
chief disturber of the peace; and because New England apprehends this result from secession, it has
from the commencement of hostilities been loudest
in its denunciations of secession, and the most zealous
advocate of a vigorous war.   At the same time, it
may be remembered that up to this moment the
contractors and manufacturers of New England have
reaped the principal benefits of the war.   From the
above it will appear that nothing else could be expected, than that the North should make every possible effort to prevent the actual accomplishment of
separation by the Southern States.

Having examined the nature of the war on the part of the North, it follows, naturally, that South resists these attacks in order to secure its independence and liberty. It has already been intimated how much the North was favoured above the South whilst the Union existed; how after the election of a 'Republican' President the apprehensions of the South reached their culmination, lest it should be handed over to the tender mercies of Northern plunderers; and how these apprehensions aroused the feelings of the Southerners at the commencement of the conflict, although they endeavoured, by every honourable means in their power, to arrange the difficulty without a resort to arms. The developements of the war have proven that these apprehensions were only too well founded, and that the fears of the Southerners that their constitutional rights and liberty would be trampled in the dust by a 'Republican' Administration, were equally well grounded. It is notorious that the liberty of the press, which had ever been regarded as the protector of the rights of the people against tyranny, has been trodden under foot in the North; that more than *eighty* of the most influential and respectable newspapers of the North have been suppressed, because they dared to advocate peace and moderation; that President Lincoln has, without any authority, wantonly suspended the privilege of the writ of habeas corpus;

that innocent men and defenceless women have been arrested by *lettres de cachet*, and incarcerated in loathsome dungeons upon mere suspicion, without an idea of the charge against them — in spite of the constitution, which provides that no one shall be deprived of liberty without ' due process of law;' that judges of the courts have been imprisoned, because, as in duty bound, they dared to vindicate the 'majesty of the law.' The President has dispersed the legislature of Maryland, a State proclaimed by himself to be loyal, and imprisoned a number of its members, because they presumed to assemble in the legitimate way prescribed by law; and he has suppressed the voice of the people at the ballot-box by an armed force, threatening to imprison all who dared to vote against the candidates of his own party, and placing soldiery at the polls to execute the threat. Cities have been burned; towns and villages have been pillaged; innocent men have been barbarously murdered; the country has been ravaged; harbours have been destroyed; and finally it has been attempted to kindle a servile war by inciting the slaves to insurrection. In a word, the South has seen constitutional liberty perish in the North, and arbitrary despotism and tyranny spring up to take its place.

In view of these facts, may it not justly be claimed that the South is carrying on a war for *order*, and for *constitutional liberty and independence*? The people of the Southern States are determined to be independent, and, convinced of the justice of their cause, are united as one man, resolved to perish all together rather than submit to the tyranny of Northern rule. If anything is potent to cause a people to fight with confidence and perfect self-devotion, it is the consciousness that they are fighting for their liberty, their homes, and their honour. This conviction pervades the entire people of the South, and is fully attested by their unity, self-sacrifice, and courage.

IV. *Contradictions in the representations made respecting the motives for waging the war.*

It is not true that the abolition of slavery in the South is the motive for the war waged by the North. At no time has this been true; and there are no facts in the case to sustain such an assumption. From the beginning of the war, the Northern press has, with the exception of the notoriously fanatical sheets, never ceased to protest that there was no intention of interfering with the institution of slavery. It is not denied, however, that the Radical portion of the press has proclaimed, with equal emphasis, the desire of the extreme Abolitionists to see slavery receive its death-blow; but this has partaken, with few exceptions, rather of the nature of a party ma-

nœuvre to excite the mob, in order thus to acquire
an influence over the Administration, and has served
to avert attention from the fact that there was no real
occasion for the war.

The North does not even desire to see slavery
abolished throughout the Southern States; but only
in the more northern of them—the Border States—as
Delaware, Maryland, Virginia, North Carolina, Tennessee, Kentucky, and Missouri. Even here, the
motive for desiring it is only to obtain fresh fields of
labour for the white working classes; for it is known
that if the slaves were emancipated, in some of these
States at least, where the climate is temperate, white
labourers would drive them from the country. As
it now is, free labour is not able to compete with
slave labour in those States.

On the other hand, every obstacle is thrown in the
way of free negroes wishing to emigrate to Northern
States; indeed, many of the States have special laws
preventing free negroes altogether from coming into
them to reside; and President Lincoln has proposed
to Congress to acquire a piece of territory beyond the
limits of the United States, whither the whole African race in America may be transported. Briefly
expressed, the abolition of slavery in America means
nothing but *more room and greater advantages for the
white labourer.*

Philanthropy is not, therefore, the spring of action

with the Northern abolitionist, as is so ostentatiously
trumpeted forth to Europe, but self-interest; for, indeed, his philanthropy is so limited that he will not
associate, or work in company, with the negro.

But self-interest is sufficient to prevent the North
from really desiring to see slavery abolished throughout the South; without African slave labour in the
unhealthy climate of that section, where it is impossible for the white man to work, the cultivation of
cotton would cease, and, thus, the cotton manufactures of the North would perish if made dependent
upon cotton produced by the labour of free blacks—
a race that notoriously will not work without compulsion. The New England manufacturer is fully
aware of this fact, and feels that he has as great an
interest in the preservation of the system of Southern
labour as the planter. But, apart from this consideration, it is, in fact, only the extreme Abolition or
' Republican ' party that pretends to wage war upon
slavery; the ' Democratic' party, although not pro-
slavery, has ever respected the rights of the South.

Repeatedly has the Government at Washington
declared that it had neither the *intention*, nor the
wish to interfere with slavery; and Mr. Lincoln has
at different times given assurance that he did not
purpose attacking the institution, seeing that he had
no power to do so under the constitution; but that
he made war for the preservation of the ' Union as

it was,' and along with it slavery. We know that General Fremont was, for the sole reason that he had presumed to declare the slaves of all ' rebel masters ' in Missouri free, deprived of his command by President Lincoln.

During the summer of 1861, Congress, in declaring that all slaves which had been employed for military service by their 'rebel masters' should be considered free, did not dare to proclaim the emancipation of *all* the slaves, not even when their owners were serving in the ' rebel army.' Another evidence of the disposition of the North originally not to meddle with slavery, may be found in the Act of Congress of March 3, 1861, which provides :—' That no amendment shall be made to the constitution which will authorise or give Congress power to abolish or interfere within any State with the domestic institutions thereof, including that of persons held to labour or servitude by the laws of said State.' Here is a clear acknowledgement that no such power had been conferred by the constitution upon Congress.

How false and hypocritical, then, has been the policy of the Washington Government in exerting itself to produce the impression through its agents in Europe, that the annihilation of the accursed system of slavery is the object of the present war ! No one can fail to perceive the motive for such a policy; it was in order to obtain in this way the sympathy and moral support of Europe for a cause, which could not possibly recommend itself otherwise to the European public.

The war-cry of the Federal Government at home has always been 'the Union.' What is the true significance of the oft-repeated assertion, that 'the war is waged for the preservation of the Union?' The idea that the North is fighting for the Union from an innate, patriotic love for it, is without any foundation; otherwise efforts would have been made to preserve it by conciliation. The late Senator Douglas, in a speech in the Senate of the United States on January 3, 1861, observed —

'A war between eighteen States on the one side and fifteen on the other is to me a revolting thing. For what purpose is the war to be waged? Certainly not for the purpose of preserving the Union. You cannot expect to exterminate ten millions of people, whose passions are excited with the belief that you mean to invade their homes, and light the flames of insurrection in their midst. You must expect to exterminate, or subjugate them, or else, when you have got tired of war, to make a treaty with them. No matter whether the war lasts one year, or seven years, or thirty years, it must have an end at some time. Sooner or later both parties will become tired and exhausted; and when rendered incapable of fighting any longer, they will make a treaty of peace,

and that treaty will be one of separation. . . .
I don't understand, then, how a man can claim to be
a friend of the Union, and yet be in favour of waging
war against ten millions of people in the Union.
*You cannot cover it up much longer under the pretext of
love for the Union* . . . But where there is a
deep-rooted discontent pervading ten millions of
people, penetrating every man, woman, and child,
and involving everything dear to them, it is time for
inquiring whether there is not some cause for the
feeling.'

If the expression, 'war for the Union,' has any
meaning at all, it must signify a war for the preservation of the territory and power of the United
States. A war for this purpose, as we have already
demonstrated, is both wicked and unconstitutional,
because it is aimed against State-sovereignty, the
fundamental principle of the Union. It must, then,
be a war of conquest, and a revolutionary war on the
part of the North, since it proposes the overthrow of
existing rights by violence. The South, by fighting
against these revolutionary ideas, gives proof of its
truly conservative policy.

CHAPTER IV.

CAPACITY OF BOTH PARTIES FOR CARRYING ON THIS WAR.

I. *Resources in Men.*

UPON the commencement of hostilities, the Federal Government warned the friendly powers of Europe not to recognise the Southern States, as the rebellion would be crushed in a few weeks; and at home, too, many proclamations in the same sense were issued to the Northern public, in order to prevent sympathy for the South from developing itself in their midst. It was assumed that the North, having greater resources in men and the material of war than the South, would inevitably be successful in the contest.

Has the North fulfilled the engagement thus entered into with Europe? Not at all. On the contrary, the condition of the Federal Government has become worse with every day; for the suppression of the rebellion must take place in the insurrectionary territory, and the Northern army can scarcely be said to have more than set foot upon this up to the present time. If the bold suppressor of rebellion is not able to invade the country in which the insurrection rages, then the above-mentioned promise to crush it must be regarded as unmeaning boasting; the incapacity of the North to execute these threats, which manifests itself more clearly from day to day, allows the enemy time to arm, to gain strength, to erect works of defence, and to stand prepared with means sufficient for resistance, whenever the moment shall arrive in which the effort to crush 'the rebellion' shall be attempted. Every day of delay only adds strength to the rebels, whilst diminishing the chances of success for the invader.

The results of the war up to this time may be definitely ascertained by an examination of the two campaigns now ended. The first ended with the winter of 1861 and 1862, the second with the present winter. At the end of the first, which lasted eight months, the North had already succeeded in demonstrating its inability to subjugate the South; the Confederate army had successfully checked the advance of the Federal forces along the whole line from Missouri to Virginia, and had repulsed every attempt of the invader to penetrate into Southern territory; at the close of the operations, the Federal army retreated from Missouri to St. Louis, abandoning the entire State, with the exception of that city, to the Confederates; they also retreated before the Southern army in Kentucky; after failing to accomplish any result in Western Virginia, they were forced to retire to the extreme limit of that State, and to go into winter quarters at Wheeling; and, after two gigantic efforts to penetrate into Eastern Virginia, they were both times fearfully routed at Bull Run and Ball's Bluff, and driven back to the borders of Virginia, where they were at the commencement of the campaign. Thus it appears that during eight months the South repelled invasion from every part of its territory, recovering all the ground which had been occupied by the enemy, except certain forts that had been garrisoned by Federal forces before the commencement of the war. In the victories at Great Bethel, Bull Run, Springfield, Lexington, Ball's Bluff, and Belmont, may be perceived the successful resistance which was opposed to the Northern invasion.

But what did the North accomplish during this period? Beyond Hatteras and Port Royal, absolutely nothing. The first of these two points is only a sand-bank, which was of no importance for the enemy, not being tenable during the winter, on account of the high tides and storms which prevail at that season; and, without the occupation of the other points of the coast of North Carolina, this point would not suffice to cut off communication with the sea. Port Royal is the entrance to the harbour of Beaufort, and the possession of it only serves to render the blockade of this port effectual. The occupation of isolated points on the coast brings little advantage to the North, unless such points are to be used as bases for operations against the interior. Unfortunately for the North, its ships were not able to sail on dry land; and with large armies it had vainly attempted to achieve any results against Southern troops, although, in all cases in which it was essayed, the attending circumstances were far more favourable to the North than to the South.

The second campaign opened with the movement of the Federal land-forces under McClellan in the East, and Buell in the West; while several naval expeditions were sent against points on the coast, and the fleet of gun-boats commenced to descend the Mississippi. No success attended McClellan's attempt to advance on Richmond by Manassas, and consequently his base of operations were changed to Fort Monroe. At the same time two Federal armies advanced under Fremont from Wheeling, and under Banks from Winchester. These were both routed and almost annihilated by the Confederate forces under Jackson, who thereby freed a large part of Virginia from invasion. The result of McClellan's operations before Richmond are well-known; and the fate of the army under Pope at the second battle of Bull Run needs no further mention. The Confederates, victorious at all points in Virginia, advanced r>14   THE SECOND WAR OF INDEPENDENCE.

into Maryland, and captured Harper's Ferry with
its garrison and immense military stores. Subsequently, a drawn battle was fought at Antietam,
which left the Federal army in almost the same condition as after the first battle of Bull Run, and no
further advanced into Virginia. In the West, the
campaign commenced under auspices peculiarly
favourable to the North; it had completed its fleet
of gun-boats for operations on the rivers, whilst its
army was composed of the best men, probably, in the
service, being chiefly trained German soldiers. The
advance of these combined forces was successful at
first: Fort Donnelson fell, and thus the way was
opened for the gun-boats to Nashville. The Confederate lines were broken, and the sense of security
which had sprung up from the results of the first
campaign was impaired. Previously it had been the
policy of the Confederates to defend the entire extent
of their frontiers; the local interests and demands of
the different States rendered this at first necessary.
It now became evident, however, that the North was
preparing for a long war; the necessity of employing
their forces in the most available manner dictated to
the Confederates the expediency of changing the
general idea of the campaign; and it was, accordingly, decided to concentrate the forces dispersed
over such a great extent of country. With this
change in their plans, the Confederate forces succes-

sively evacuated several positions in Kentucky and Tennessee, retiring to the new lines of defence further southwards. The Federals continued their advance to Shiloh, where the western army received a shock from the Confederates under Beauregard and Johnson, from which it has never recovered. Since that time the Federal army in the West, divided into several corps, has been marching and counter-marching in that section—at one time pursuing, and again the pursued. Although several battles have been fought in that region since Beauregard's celebrated retreat, they have generally been between comparatively small forces on both sides; and while neither army has obtained complete possession of Kentucky, the Confederates retain at least as much as they possessed of that State at the commencement of the war. The Federal forces which had advanced under cover of their gun-boats into Alabama, have been driven back entirely; and Tennessee is free from the Federals, with the exception of Nashville and country round Memphis, both of which are held by gun-boats. West of the Mississippi the operations have been attended with varied results for both armies; but they have been unimportant by reason of the small numbers engaged, thus effecting in no way materially the final issue of the war.

Turning to the naval operations, we find that they have been limited to the occupation of a number of

points of minor importance on the coast, which have
rendered the blockade more effective; and to the
capture of New Orleans, and a part of the Mississippi
river, Vicksburg having resisted successfully all
attacks made upon it. Thus we see that after
another year of war, the North is as far from the
accomplishment of its object as at the commencement of hostilities; the conquest of the South is
no more nearly achieved than before it was attempted; the South has lost no points essential to
defence; communication between the States has
been maintained, and many new ways of communication opened; no single State has been subjugated,
nor do the Federals rule over any portions of
Southern territory, except those actually occupied
for the moment by their forces; in a word, nothing
essential to the success of the South has been lost,
and, indeed, the results of this second campaign are
largely in its favour.

On the breaking out of hostilities, the Government of Lincoln announced that by December 1,
1861, the Federal army would be in possession of
Richmond, Charleston, Mobile, New Orleans, and
Nashville. Only two of these cities, New Orleans,
and Nashville, are occupied by the Federals, and
these were taken by the navy, not by the army.

Whence, then, this over-estimation of its means on
the part of the Northern? The response is that,

although the North is very rich, and contains a larger population, the South is not without great resources; while a variety of circumstances conspire to render a large proportion of the Northern population unavailable for an aggressive war.

In regard to the population of the two belligerent powers, we extract the following from the official census of 1860, published by the Department of State at Washington. The entire population of the South, with the exception of Delaware, is thus specified : —

	Free inhabitants .	Slave inhabitants
Alabama	529,164	435,132
Arkansas	324,323	111,104
Florida	78,686	61,753
Georgia	595,079	462,230
Kentucky	930,223	225,490
Louisiana	376,913	332,520
Maryland	599,846	87,188
Mississippi	354,699	436,696
Missouri	1,058,352	114,965
North Carolina	661,586	331,081
South Carolina	301,271	402,541
Tennessee	834,063	275,784
Texas	420,651	180,388
Virginia .	1,105,196	490,887
District of Columbia	71,895	3,181
Total	8,241,965	3,950,940

To this must be added the territory of New Mexico, the entire free population of which amounts to 93,517 souls, which with the above 8,241,965 make a total of 8,335,482. But the entire free

population of the United States in 1860 was
27,477,090; so that, after subtracting the 8,335,482
inhabitants of the South, there remains a population of
19,141,608 in the North.

These numbers, 8,335,482 and 19,141,608 respectively, must not be assumed as absolutely accurate in the examination of the resources of the
two sections; for there is, in certain of the seceded
States, a portion of the population disaffected towards
the South, as in Missouri, Kentucky, Maryland, and
small districts in Tennessee and Virginia, from which
contingents for the Northern army have been taken;
while in several of the Northern States, there is a
large proportion of the inhabitants which sym-
pathises with the Confederates, and has refused to
contribute soldiers for the war. Still it may be
assumed, without essential error, that the number of
the 'disaffected' on each side is about the same,
although no troops have been furnished by Cali-
fornia and Utah, and few by certain parts of Indiana, Illinois, and Delaware. It must be borne
in mind, however, that only a certain proportion of
these respective numbers are capable of bearing
arms; that these are persons of the age which
furnishes the principal class of labourers; that, necessarily, a large number of men capable of bearing
arms in the North must remain at home for the
cultivation of the soil; whilst in the South this

labour is performed almost exclusively by the slaves, whereby the entire male population capable of bearing arms can be spared for the army. Another consideration of no little significance is the amount of labour done by the negro slaves. In the South the slaves of both sexes are employed, the females working in the fields as well as ' in-doors.' The negro children, too, are not left without employment of a light kind. In the North, on the other hand, the white females are employed only with their domestic concerns, or in the factories, and the children must spend a part of their time in the schools. It will thus be obvious, that the amount of agricultural labour done by 4,000,000 of slaves in the South is, *cæteris paribus*, much greater than that performed by a white population of the same numbers in the North. For these reasons, the difference in the number of men that may be spared for the army from both sections respectively is nothing like so great, as the disproportion of population would, at first sight, appear to indicate.

II. *The Navy.*

It cannot be denied that the North possesses in its navy an immense superiority over the South. Almost the whole of the former navy of the United States remained in the hands of the North; though its efficiency was considerably impaired by the large number of Southern naval officers that resigned upon the secession of their respective States.

But little discernment is necessary to discover that, with a navy like that of the North, under ordinary circumstances, immense injury may be inflicted upon another commercial power. From this point of view, however, the South has but little to fear, not possessing a commercial navy which the armed navy of the North might destroy. The action of the Northern navy is, then, limited to two fields of operation; the one to maintain a blockade of the Southern ports, the other for hostilities against the seaport cities. One of the first measures of war undertaken by the North was the proclamation of a blockade of the entire coast of the seceded States. At that time the navy was notoriously insufficient for keeping up an effective blockade of a coast, with an extent of more than 2,400 miles, abounding in bays and creeks, which are navigable only for ships of light tonnage. The difficulty of such an undertaking, with even a much larger navy than that with which the North set the blockade on foot, cannot fail to be perceived by everyone; for the almost numberless points of entrance for ships would render any but a navy of the first class totally incompetent. According to the international law of Europe, as laid down in the protocol of Paris, a blockade to be binding must be effective. That the blockade of the Southern States for a long time could not pretend to be anything like effective, is evident from the fact that, between the proclamation of it and the following month of November, more than five hundred ships of all sizes did successfully pass through it; while the number of captures made during the same period was altogether inconsiderable. Was it not, therefore, pure forbearance on the part of the European powers to have acknowledged and respected the paper-blockade for so long a time? In the desperate effort to render the blockade of the Southern ports real, by sinking vessels laden with stone in the harbours, a tangible evidence was afforded of the incapacity of the Federal Government to accomplish what it had undertaken. No comment is necessary upon the infamy of this proceeding, which, by subjecting the North to the just execration of the civilised world, has been far more injurious to its cause than to the harbours of the South.

The Federal Government perceived at an early day the advantages that might result from a fleet of gunboats, operating on the great rivers that traverse the South in every direction; the navy-yards and docks were in their own hands, and every facility for rapidly constructing a river-navy was at their disposal. Accordingly, we find that no time was lost in the execution of this project; in less than a year a large number of gun-boats, some iron-cased, started down the Mississippi, cooperating with the land-forces. The first victory achieved by this new arm of the service was the capture of Fort Donnelson. But in the meantime the regular navy of the North has been increased to such an extent, that the blockade is no longer a purely paper one, though certainly not perfect; at all events, the favourable moment for ceasing to respect it, when it was notoriously ridiculous, has glided out of the hands of the Great Powers of Europe. The indulgence accorded to an insolent power is now reacting upon the nations that granted it.

For all purposes of naval warfare the South can scarcely be said to possess any means of resistance to the North. Still, important results for defence have been achieved by the improvised navy of the South. The exploits of the 'Virginia' ('Merrimac') and 'Arkansas' are familiar; whilst the damage inflicted on Northern commerce by the 'Sumter,' 'Nashville,' and 'Alabama' is clearly visible in the rates of insurance demanded for Northern vessels. Indeed, the insecurity of Northern commerce is already so great, that trade between America and Europe is being rapidly transferred to English bottoms. Here, then, is the vulnerable part of the Northern navy, and the South will endeavour to profit by it. Nevertheless, the inequality existing between the two belligerents in this branch of the

resources of war, is too great to justify the hope of
its being removed within any short period; yet the
South is making every effort to remove the difficulty
under which it labours.

III. *Material Resources.*

It has already been observed that in the North the
army has to be recruited from the male population
between the ages of eighteen and forty-five years,
the same body of men that constitute the usual
labouring classes. The whole of this population
must render military duty on occasion, it is true;
but the wealthy classes are virtually exempt, because
it is at their option to procure substitutes. Consequently, the soldiers must chiefly consist of actual
labourers. Now, these are composed of the agricultural classes, the operatives, and those in the cities
employed in various commercial callings. As regards
the quality of an army composed of such material,
it will be conceded that the strongest and ablest
soldiers are always those accustomed to out-door
pursuits—the cultivators of the soil. But just this
population is least of all represented in the Northern
army. The manner of recruiting makes this almost
inevitable. When a certain number of troops are to
be raised, they are apportioned to the different

States; and the Governor of each State is then called upon to raise the quota assigned to it. Hereupon the Governor issues a call for volunteers; and it is only when these are not forthcoming that the conscription is put in force. But as in time of war the natural tendency of agricultural products is to become dearer, the occupation of agriculture becomes more profitable, and agricultural labour accordingly advances in price. This circumstance tends to prevent such labourers from enlisting in the army. On the other hand, the numerous factories which have been closed on account of the want of a supply of material, and of markets for manufactured articles, have been forced to discharge their operatives. Thus a very large class without employment has been thrown upon the North; and of these the army has, in a great degree, been composed. Inactivity in trade, also, has turned vast numbers out of employment in the cities. Rather than starve, large numbers from these two classes of the population have been induced to enter the army to obtain a support. Yet this has not been unattended with symptoms pregnant of trouble for the Government. The recruits have in many instances given visible evidence of a disposition to force the Federal Government to do more than pay for their services. Meetings have been held, and resolutions passed, declaring it to be the duty of the Government to support the starving families of

its soldiers.   Nor has the Government been able to
extricate itself from the difficulty; in the form of
unprecedented bounties, the Government has been
compelled to acquiesce in demands made upon it.
But the continuation of this is dependent upon the
ability to pay the bounties.   As long as the Federal
Government has credit, it can continue to pay its
soldiers; but as soon as this fails, it will be seen that
the patriotism of the North will not be sufficient to
fill up the thinned ranks of its army.   Conscription
may be resorted to, as already decided upon some
months since, but the obstacles to its execution will
be found almost insuperable.   Wherever it has been
attempted to enforce it as yet, violent resistance has
been offered and bloody riots have occurred.   Thus
all will depend upon the finances of the North.   Love
for the Union may be never so strong in the North:
but men love their wives and children more; they
will not leave these at home to starve, and the interests
of self-preservation will triumph.   In this way the
North may find itself compelled to terminate the
war, in order to prevent revolution at home.

Trade is now stagnant, except in the necessaries
for carrying on the war.   The finances of the North
are also tottering and must soon crumble; the expenses of the war are daily increasing, and no means
of defraying them have been devised.   It is true that
the Federal Congress has passed laws for levying a

direct tax, but not a dollar has been raised in this way as yet.

At the commencement of the war the banks were the supporters of the Government; indeed, they had no choice, for their very existence was in the hands of a lawless government. But, with an outlay of 20,000,000*l.* per month, the resources of the banks were soon exhausted. Resort was then had to a 'popular loan,' which, with the duties raised by the Morrill tariff-bill, still failed to supply the steadily increasing demands of the Government. Long before the expenses of the war became so enormous, at the time of the discussion of the budget for the financial year from July 1861 to 1862, Mr. Chase estimated the necessary expenses at 109,000,000*l.*; of this sum only 66,000,000*l.* had been provided for by the ingenious devices of the Secretary of the Treasury. According to Mr. Chase's statements, he expected at that time a deficit of 43,000,000*l.* for the first year of the war; and he confessed that only 6,400,000*l.* could be hoped for from duties.

But the patriotism, wealth, and banks of the North were not sufficient. Mr. Chase was finally compelled to propose a direct tax, which, it was calculated, would yield 4,000,000*l.*, and an income tax producing 2,000,000*l.* more. Still the execution of the law imposing these taxes has not yet been attempted; but when the taxgatherer does commence to make his calls, and put his finger in the pockets of the Yankee, the latter will soon cry Peace, unless he shall have changed his nature.

One of Mr. Chase's first schemes for raising a part of the 43,000,000*l.* wanting, was to substitute for the circulating medium of the banks a Federal currency to the amount of 30,000,000*l.*, which should be convertible into Federal securities. It was proposed, on the one hand, to substitute worse securities for the existing ones of the bank-currencies; whilst, on the other, the destruction of the financial systems in the individual States must have been the result. How this plan could have improved the state of affairs we have never been able to discover.

Finally, Congress made Federal paper a legal tender with a forced circulation. Thus at last Mr. Chase was enabled to meet his demands, finding it incomparably easier to print money than to raise it by taxation. Gradually the expenses of the war have increased to such an extent that these facilities for creating money do not suffice. At first this system worked well enough, but repeated issues of paper caused the new legal tender to depreciate. Paper still retains its nominal value, if you please; but gold has advanced by reason of the ' cheapness of money.' As might easily have been anticipated, the result of such a reckless system of finance has been to flood the country with a currency now worth

only about two-thirds of its nominal value, and to
drive gold and silver out of circulation.

According to the best means of judging, the
debt of the Federal Government already exceeds
400,000,000*l.*, and is increasing at the rate of
20,000,000*l.* per month; while no way of raising
an amount for paying the interest on it has been
discovered. Well may the financial system of the
Federal Government be designated as reckless and
ruinous. It is attempted to obtain money for conducting the war by loan, or otherwise; but no adequate measures are adopted for paying the interest or
gradually discharging the debt. Certainly it does
appear as if the Government only tried to satisfy
present want, leaving the future to take care of itself.

Sooner or later resort must be had to a foreign
loan; but this will be attended with no result, for
the capitalists of Europe are not inclined to take
the risk of such a loan, made by the Federal Government upon the faith of thirty-four States, when,
under the most fortunate circumstances, it must be
borne by twenty States. There is no confidence
felt in Europe in the administration of the Federal
finances, for reasons just given; besides, all the
efforts made to dispose of Federal securities in
Europe since the war have proved fruitless. In
fact, the Government of Washington is already
bankrupt, although every effort is made to conceal

it. This state of affairs cannot last much longer, for the true condition will ere long be known everywhere. Moreover, who would be disposed to lend money to the Union, when there is every reason to believe that, in the event of a war with one of the European powers, the private capital possessed by it in American funds would be confiscated?

What a different picture does the South present! Here all personal interests are forgotten in the sacrifices made for the public weal. The Southerners are firmly united, resolved, if necessary, to sacrifice everything to the attainment of their independence.

None of the statements made about the starving of the Southern people have any foundation in truth; for the South is an agricultural region which produces not only enough cereals and other means of subsistence for its own use, but exports, as every well-informed person is aware, large quantities to the North and abroad. The income from its exports of meal, rice, beans, wheat, hogs, and cattle is very considerable. Any one acquainted with the varied nature of the soil of the South knows that it is simply absurd to reason about the danger of the South starving; more especially now that the export of its productions has ceased, whereas the quantity has increased, the war having had little influence to derange the system of involuntary labour.

Whoever may be disposed to doubt these statements is referred to the statistics of the United States, carefully collated by Mr. Hopkins * in his introduction to the 'South Vindicated.' The South possesses also minerals in abundance, as iron and lead; as well as a number of excellent manufactories of arms. The foundries of Richmond were among the most celebrated in America, and the best cannon furnished to the Federal Government were manufactured there. These, with others in different parts of the South, are now capable of supplying all the necessities of the Government. The South, although possessing considerable munitions of war on the commencement of hostilities, was not as well provided with them as the Northern Government then asserted; nor were these by any means sufficient for a war of the magnitude of the present one. But since that time large numbers of arms have been imported from Europe, despite the blockade; these, with the supplies manufactured at home, and the enormous quantities captured from the enemy, leave the South in no want of arms at this time.

No reference has been made to the armament of the North before, because it was self-evident that with its navy any quantity of munitions might be obtained from Europe, as long as the peace was not interrupted. Now, however, the 'Alabama' has

* Williams, 'The South Vindicated,' pp. xli.—xlv.

appeared on the stage of action, by which event the certainty of obtaining supplies from Europe has been jeopardised.   Indeed, it is asserted that the North, having lost such immense military stores during the war, is at present sadly in want of arms for its new levies.   All kinds of munitions are now manufactured in the South, so that the blockade is incapable of inflicting vital injury in that direction.

Undoubtedly, the South has suffered much from the blockade; but the representations made by the North of the suffering in the Southern army for clothing and the means of subsistence, are gross exaggerations.   For reasons already intimated, the Southern soldiers demand only arms and support, and a large proportion of them refuse to accept any pay whatever from the Government; while thousands of wealthy officers and privates have united to defray the whole expense of the organization and support of entire regiments.   Every house contributes to the comfort of the soldiers, and there is no reason that the army should suffer from any great want.   Convinced that the war is prosecuted for their own interests and welfare, the Southerners vie with each other in the liberality of their contributions for the support of their defenders, and for the aid of the Government, in order to relieve it of as much expense as possible.   For it is quite indifferent whether the means for the support of the army, or money for

obtaining them, be contributed; in the first instance
the necessity for money is in a great degree obviated.
An example of the extent of the voluntary aid
afforded to the Government in the form of articles
of subsistence, may be seen in the contributions
from the city of New Orleans during the month of
October before its capture; these amounted to
200,000*l.*, and were designed exclusively for the
army in Virginia, account being taken of no contribution under the value of 20*l.* Articles of luxury
are, then, the principal things, of which much want
is felt.

It has already been mentioned that the system of
involuntary labour in the South has not been de-
ranged by the war.   It may. now be added that
before the commencement of hostilities, as constantly
since, the North has threatened the South with a
slave insurrection; on the breaking out of the war,
or latest upon the approach of a Northern army, the
slaves, it was asserted, would rise, murder their
masters, and burn their houses. The Southerners
have never feared such a result; and experience has
confirmed their opinions, while proving the error of
the North.   As long ago as November 1861, the
'Journal of Commerce,' a New York organ of Lincoln's party, confessed the hopelessness of expect-
ing the cooperation of the slaves. It spoke as follows : —

'General Halleck has issued orders, that in consequence of important information respecting the numbers and condition of our forces being conveyed to the enemy by fugitive slaves, no such person shall hereafter be permitted to enter the lines of any camp, or any forces on the march, and any now within such lines to be immediately excluded therefrom. * * * At fortress Monroe too, it was discovered very soon after the breaking out of hostilities that the negroes were secretly giving information to the enemy. If this is the way the black population of the South serve the cause of the Union, the less we have of them the better. * * * In the many discussions which the slave-question has brought about, there has not as yet been elicited a particle of evidence that the slaves of the South would accept freedom and arms, or would fight for the Union against their masters.'

Apart from the well-known devotion and attachment of the slaves to their masters, a slave-insurrection would be impossible, on account of the absence of all means of communication between the plantations; but were a general conspiracy conceivable, the execution of it would be impracticable, for the slaves have no arms; and if they had arms, they would not know how to use them. We do not deny that in remote sections the presence of a Northern army might be able to intimidate many slaves, and induce others to commit barbarities, but these would be rare exceptions. Moreover, the Northern army has so far demonstrated its inability to penetrate into the interior, in order to place arms in the hands of the slaves.

Upon comparing the financial system of the South with that of the North, we are struck with the contrast between the amounts of their respective debts, and the rates of monthly expenditure. The debt of the Confederate States amounts to 69,000,000l. against 400,000,000l. on the part of the United States; the monthly expenditure of the former is about 5,000,000l., while that of the latter is 20,000,000l. But the chief difference between the two systems consists in the fact that the South has resolved to raise by direct taxation the means necessary for conducting the war. To this the Southerners readily submit, because the nature of their productions is such that they can support a much higher rate of taxation than the North. A few years of prosperity after the war will suffice to remove all traces of the temporary sufferings produced by it.

In conclusion, the South is by no means in such a forlorn condition as has been depicted; but were its condition never so bad, the Southerners are determined to endure every privation, rather than submit to the North; they have made this a popular war, in which every individual is directly interested.

IV. *Army-Organization.*

One of the principal causes of the numerous defeats which the Northern army has experienced, and of the corresponding successes of the Southern army, lies in the difference of their respective organization.

In the North the suppression of the 'rebellion' was at first regarded as a thing of no great difficulty, as seen in the fact that Lincoln limited his first call for men to seventy-five thousand. It will be remembered how volunteers flocked to Washington, in response to this call, for a three months' service in the district of Columbia in defence of the capital. The behaviour of these volunteers, a few days before they were led on Manassas, is familiar to all. Several regiments ran away the day before the battle, and others still left the field during the battle, and marched home, because their term of service had expired on that day. The North profited by this experience, and recruited its subsequent levies for three years; but still the other great defects of organization were not remedied by this act.

We repeat only the statements of the press, and of the officers of the regular army of the North, when we characterize the discipline of the Federal army as entirely unworthy of respect. There exists a lawless spirit throughout, and an impatience of subordination

that amounts too often to mutiny. Between the
officers and soldiers of the old regular army and
those of the militia, there is an irreconcilable enmity;
and constant difficulties are arising out of the impla-
cable hatred between the native-born and naturalized
soldiers.   The Northern Government asserts that the
men composing its army are not to be surpassed in
the qualities proper to a soldier; whereas throughout
the army the absence of subordination and respect
for superiors, and the want of warlike pride and a
military spirit, are notorious.   The prevalence of
drunkenness, the general disposition to dissipation,
and the slight appreciation of the point of honour, so
indispensable to the soldier, are qualities appertaining
to the majority of the Northern soldiers.   From the
beginning of the war there has been notoriously a
great want of competent officers for training the
troops; the volunteers are commanded chiefly by
civilians and politicians, who have entered the army
to acquire political influence; the ignorance of the
men in the use of arms constitutes a serious difficulty
in the way of rapid organization; and, finally, the
men are not influenced by that determination and
self-devotion which animate the hearts of those
fighting for their homes.   Mob-rule, and the fact
that the army consists chiefly of men destitute of
means, and without employment, who must be paid
extravagant bounties for fighting, as well as the

established incapacity of the generals and field officers, are sufficient reasons for considering an army, so organized, totally incompetent for subjugating the South.   As might well be expected of such an army, it brings robbery, theft, violence, and murder in its train, and has left the most infamous traces of barbarism behind it, wherever it has appeared. In fact, the notion of the essential requisites of a soldier seems to be entirely unknown in the North.

When the war broke out, the North was entirely without any commissary-department and train of importance; and the Federal Government had to contend with unusual difficulties in supplying the army with arms, clothing and the means of subsistence, because it was the prey of numberless speculators, and plunderers of the public treasury.   Nor was it possible to send to Europe for better and cheaper materials, until after the last home-made articles had been exhausted; for the mob of Northern contractors and manufacturers would submit to no competition.

If we compare the Southern army with that of the North, it is not because the comparison is justifiable, but merely to exhibit the immeasurable difference between them.   With few exceptions, the Southern army has consisted all the time of troops enlisted for the war; there has been no necessity for conscription, except to regulate the number of men to be taken from the different States and counties, for it was discovered at an early day that entire districts were in danger of being depopulated. The Conscription Act as passed, and carried into operation in the South, proposed only to make the burden of military service uniform.

There has been no lack of competent and able field and regimental officers in the Southern army. Formerly there was a large number of Southern officers in the Federal army, but these remaining loyal to their respective States, resigned their commissions, and entered the service of the Confederate States. It is not denied, even by the North, that the best officers of the old regular army were these same Southerners.

Little need be said about the skill of the Southern generals. This has formed the theme of admiration in Europe ever since the breaking out of the war; and they have won the respect of the most distinguished military men in the whole world. Their ability has been attested most fully in the results of the battles that have been fought.

A well-known assertion of the North was that the Southerners would not submit to strict military discipline. Experience has proved the contrary, and the South exhibits in its army, consisting to a great extent of the best and wealthiest citizens, a picture almost without a parallel in history. The Southerners

have, from infancy, been accustomed to the use of
arms, and to live a great deal in the open air; habit-
uated to govern their slaves, they have learnt the
importance of subordination, and therefore subject
themselves with the greatest ease and willingness to
the severe discipline of the army. Mutiny and everything approaching to it are unknown in the Southern
army; whereas it is notorious that, in repeated instances, entire regiments in the Northern army have
been disarmed and disbanded on this account; and
the Northern press, fettered as it is, still gives frequent information of instances in which soldiers or
officers have shot their superiors.   Cases of this kind
are unheard of in the South.

Although the want of a train has been felt in the
South, still the necessity for it is not so great as in
the North. The want has partially been supplied;
to this the stores captured from the enemy have contributed no inconsiderable part. Unfortunately, the
seat of war is on Southern soil, but this obviates the
pressing necessity for a train adapted to the wants of
an invading army; moreover, the network of rail-
roads which form the internal means of communication and transportation, supply to a considerable
degree the ordinary demand for a train.

In connexion with the enthusiasm of the Southern
army, there exists on the part of the troops unlimited
confidence in the capacity of their leaders, as well as

K

in their own superiority over the Northern soldiers. Nor have the results of the two campaigns now ended, in which the North has accomplished nothing of importance, failed to establish an immense superiority for the South. The capacity of both armies will, however, be judged by their performances; and from this point of view the Southern army has no reason to envy the army of the North.

V. *Duration of the War.*

From the foregoing considerations, it may be assumed, we think, that, although the South must necessarily suffer many disadvantages from a war of such magnitude, yet it possesses the capacity and the means for conducting a war of defence for an almost unlimited time. The North, on the other hand, is forced to terminate the war in a decided manner within a short period, for its finances will soon be exhausted.

Signs of future troubles already manifest themselves unmistakably between the 'Democratic' and 'Republican' parties; and the best interpreters of public opinion in America declare that the late triumph of the former party seals the doom of Lincoln and his political associates.

There is no unity of counsel and of purpose in the cabinet of President Lincoln, the members of which are in open opposition to each other as regards the object of the war and the means to be employed in conducting it. Generals are promoted and, when defeated, are degraded, perhaps to be promoted and degraded again.

Socialism has raised its head in New England, and among the foreign population of the North.

The depressing moral influence of repeated reverses in the field and of constantly increasing poverty offers a good occasion for the developement of discord, and incites the parties against each other, causing the one to attribute their misfortunes to the other. These raging domestic dissensions indicate already clearly enough the growth, and not remote outbreak, of a revolution in the North.

Long campaigns in the South are impossible, on account of the climate; because during the excessive heats of summer warlike operations are attended by the most fearful mortality; whereas, in the more northern parts, the roads are rendered impassable for artillery and baggage almost in the beginning of winter. On the other hand, the extent of the country is so great, and its population comparatively so thin, that a short war is absolutely necessary for the invader, if anything at all is to be accomplished.

.From this examination it becomes evident why the Federal Government, in fault of an inspiring idea for the war, as exists in the South, resorts to all kinds of false pretexts to excite the popular passions, and produce an enthusiasm for the war. So we find that on the one hand the Minister for War proposes to arm the slaves, and turn them loose against their masters; on the other, the demagogues proclaim to the people that nothing can be accomplished by the war without the emancipation of the entire African race in America. This is a very open confession, but has no importance except for exciting the popular feeling. And now that the emancipation of the slaves has, in reality, been decided upon by the Republican President, the act can only be regarded as the expression of a spirit of diabolical revenge, and as an indication of unpardonable puerility, since its execution is impossible. Finally, it was for the same reason that the Washington Government spared no pains to produce the false impression among the Northern people, that the majority of the people in every Southern State, South Carolina probably excepted, were devoted to the Union, but were overpowered by an armed faction, and would welcome the approach of a Federal army. Without resort to such means of exciting the popular feeling, or without speedy victory, Lincoln will before long be compelled by the conservative party in the North to conclude a peace.

The South is aware of these facts, and knows that it has nothing to fear from a long war, because its enemy will be utterly ruined by it.

CHAPTER V.

ISSUE OF THE WAR.

FEW indeed will have the hardihood now to assert that the causes of the antipathy between the North and the South can be removed by the present war. On the contrary, the war has aroused all the just indignation of the Southerners, and excited their passions to the highest point; and not only has the former limited confidence in the North been destroyed, but, in the place of their former antipathy for the Yankees, a deadly and inextinguishable hate has sprung up.

Should the South be re-incorporated into the Union by force, it cannot be expected that the people that have waged such a ruthless war against the Southerners would ever allow them the exercise of their former constitutional rights; or that those who are now designated as traitors would ever be permitted, if so disposed, to sit in Congress, and take part in the councils of the Union with those whose loyalty has never been impeached. With the triumph of the North would vanish the former constitutional

character of the Federal Government, which was based
upon 'the consent of the governed.' The South,
foreseeing this, and having learned its strength in its
victories, is determined to offer resistance, if necessary, 'till every valley from the Rio Grande to the
Potomac shall overflow with blood, till every hill-
top shall be bleached with the bones of Southern
warriors.'

The war of 1812 with England demonstrated the
impossibility of holding such a vast territory in subjection: nor will the difficulty be less for the North
than it was for Great Britain; for the North is not
now in such a condition to wage war against the
South, as Great Britain was at that time to carry on
war with the United States. The occupation of any
point whatever will not put an end to the war; and
should the Southern army be annihilated, of which
there is little danger, the real difficulties will then
only commence. A Guerilla would be instituted, by
which the North would finally be compelled to make
peace.

At the present moment, the Government of the
Confederate States of America is conducted with
order and dignity. In the individual States the
different functions of government are exercised as
quietly as before the breaking out of the war. It
has not been found necessary to suspend the privilege of the writ of habeas-corpus, to suppress news-

papers, or to arrest and imprison individuals without trial, for the sake of preserving order.

The Confederate States exhibit the picture of a well-organised Government, which exists not only de jure, as we have tried to show, but also de facto. No intervention of the European Powers is desired by this Government to secure its permanence. It is strong enough to maintain its independence unassisted.

CHAPTER VI.

AFRICAN SLAVERY.*

I. *General Observations.*

TWENTY negroes, which were brought to Virginia in a Dutch man-of-war from Africa in 1620, formed the germ of the slave-population in the North American Republics. From this time the trade in slaves between Africa and America was continued till the year 1807. During this period slavery was introduced into all of the original thirteen States.† The entire number of slaves imported into the United States from Africa is estimated at 330,000. They belonged chiefly to the tribes of the Mandingoes, Koromantyns, Fidahs, Eboes, Fantis, Ashantis,

---

* We take pleasure in acknowledging our indebtedness to the excellent work of the Hon. T. R. R. Cobb, *An Inquiry into the Law of Negro Slavery in America* (Philadelphia and Savannah, 1858), for much accurate and scientific information respecting the history and laws of slavery in America. Those disposed to pursue their inquiries in this direction will find much that is valuable in this work to repay the trouble of consulting it.

† It is not unusual to hear it asserted that slavery never existed in Massachusetts. According to the census of 1754, there were in that State 2,448 slaves over 16 years of age, of which 1,000 were in Boston. See also Hildreth, *History of the United States*, vol. i. p, 419.

Krumen, Quaquas, and Congoes, and were held in bondage in their native country. In coming to America,
these savages only exchanged barbarian for civilized
masters. It is scarcely necessary to speak of the
sufferings of the 'middle-passage' and other enormi-
ties with which the slave-trade was attended. Within
the last half century the evils committed during the
two previous centuries have found their condemnation
among the nations that caused them. It is true, the
advantages of the cruel system had been reaped, but
it was better to abandon the 'nefarious traffic' late
than never.

After the recognition of the independence of the
United States, it was proposed by the Convention that
framed the constitution, to abolish the trade in slaves
between Africa and America. It was objected, however, that the shipping interests of the Northern
States would suffer to too great an extent, should
the trade be stopped suddenly. Massachusetts in-
sisted most strongly, along with Georgia and South
Carolina, that the trade should be continued for a few
years to come. In conformity with this proposition,
the year 1808 was fixed upon for the termination of
the slave trade. It did actually cease in 1807, one
year earlier than originally intended.

Vermont was the first State to decree the abolition
of slavery within its limits; and by the Bill of Rights
adopted in 1777 slavery was excluded from that

State.   In 1790 there were only seventeen slaves in
Vermont to take advantage of this generous measure.
Slavery was abolished successively by all the States,
until the institution was limited to the fifteen Southern
States.   Nevertheless, as late as 1840 there were
five slaves in Rhode Island, seventeen in Connecticut,
one in New Hampshire, sixty-four in Pennsylvania,
four in New York, and six hundred and seventy-four
in New Jersey.*   Slavery was abolished in all the
Northern States by 'gradual emancipation,' a period
having been fixed upon, after which all issue of the
slaves were to be free.   These plans, being all pro-
spective, allowed ample time for transporting the slaves
from the North to the Southern States, where, in fact,
most of them were sold.   Care was also taken to
fix the dates of emancipation sufficiently distant, to
avoid the depreciation in value that would have
resulted from forcing the entire slave-population of
the North upon the Southern market within too
short a space of time.   It is well known that the
gradual abolition of slavery in the North was not
the result of philanthropy; but it took place purely
from considerations of expediency; partly because
the climate had been found unadapted to the negro;
and partly on account of the comparatively limited
extent of the real estate in the hands of single individuals, which rendered the employment of small

* United States Census of 1840.

numbers of slaves less profitable than in the South, where organised labour on the plantations was extremely remunerative. Another motive was the sufficiency of white labour in the North, which by competition made slave labour too dear; whereas the scarcity of white labour in the South made the demand for slaves very great. Nor did the abolition of slavery in the North propose conferring upon the negroes an equality with the free white citizens, but consisted only in the prohibition to hold slaves after a specified time; consequently, the majority of the slaves found masters in the South, and the few that were emancipated never obtained the right of citizenship, except in Vermont. The number of slaves have increased to 3,952,801 according to the census of 1860.

Nothing is more natural than the repugnance of Europeans of the present day for the word *slavery*. When, however, the actual condition of the *African* slaves in the Southern States is examined, much of the antipathy to the system of slavery in America will be discovered to be unfounded.

Slavery in America may be considered from two points of view—on the one hand, as a *social*, on the other, as a *political* relation. Regarded from the first point of view, slavery is decidedly patriarchal. The head of the family is the slaveowner or master, while the slaves are incorporated into the family.

The wife and children excepted, the slaves claim the chief care and attention of the head of the family. Interest and feeling unite to induce the master to bestow the greatest kindness and protection upon his dependents; and, in this way, a more intimate bond of affection is created than is possible between the master and hireling in any country. The master is, at the same time, the protector, confidant, and friend of his slaves, and must afford them clothing, support, medical attention, and religious instruction. The children of the slave-proprietor grow up with those of the slaves, so that from the earliest youth there exists a mutual affection between the future master and his slaves. This is the secret of the wonderful attachment of the slave, on the one hand, to his master, and of the disinclination of the master, on the other, to part with his slaves. It is, indeed, a common thing for masters to sacrifice property of every kind, rather than be separated from their negro slaves. A tangible evidence, too, of the contentment and devotion of the slaves is to be found in the fact, that only one insurrection worthy of the name has ever taken place among then. This occurred in Virginia, as long ago as the year 1800, and was instigated by Northern abolitionists, but divulged by faithful slaves.* The world has witnessed the

* See documents in the *Richmond Recorder* of the 3rd, 6th, and 9th of April, 1803.

behaviour of the slaves during the present war; and
we venture the assertion, that not only nine-tenths of
the slaves would voluntarily fight for their masters
against the Yankees, but that the masters would feel
no hesitation or apprehension in placing arms in the
hands of their slaves for defence, should it be found
necessary. Nor can it be believed that any similar
population of the same numbers, in any part of the
world, would have remained so faithfully attached to
their superiors, when so many and so constant incen-
diary attempts had been made to seduce them from
their loyalty.

A consequence of this patriarchal relation is that
the separation of the family is rendered incomparably more difficult, and less seldom among the
negro slaves than among any other labouring class
of the world. A proof of the mildness of the system
of slavery in the Southern States is afforded by the
rapid increase in the number of the slaves; from
330,000, they have become 4,000,000, and when we
take all the circumstances into consideration, it
appears that their rate of increase has been fully
equal to that of the white population. If we look
at the free black population of the North, we shall
find that it falls far behind. According to the
seventh census, the increase of free blacks, from 1840
to 1850, was under 1½ per cent. per annum; while
that of the negro slaves was but a fraction under

3 per cent. per annum. The same authority shows
that the longevity of the Southern slaves is far
above that of the free negroes of the Northern States;
while there are 'three times as many deaf mutes,
four times as many blind, more than three times
as many idiots, and more than ten times as many
insane, in proportion to numbers, among the free
coloured persons, than among the slaves.' The
same holds good with respect to the free blacks of
Liberia. Few, probably, will be found to dispute
the assertion that the condition of the negroes under
the beneficent system of American slavery, is infinitely better than that of their own race in the
land of their origin. Although their intellectual
developement in slavery has been very much advanced, the negroes never lose the characteristics
of their race. But, above all, the moral condition
of the negroes has been improved by the ameliorating
influences of slavery. Though gay, affectionate, and
grateful, they always retain their disposition for
lust, falsehood, and theft; and while many are
consistent Christians, they never lose their super-
stitious nature, and can scarcely be made to appreciate the immoral nature of certain acts.

It is not unfrequently objected by the opponents
of slavery, that the education of their children is not
left to the slaves. However true this may be in
theory, it does not hold true in the case of the

African slaves. For, although the master allows the slave-parents the general management of their children, his authority is necessary both to give effect to that of the parents, and to interpose in case of negligence or cruelty, which are characteristic. But for this the children would only too often be the victims of the passion of their parents.

It is not denied that the objection, that marriage between the slaves is not recognised by law, is better founded; still the separation of man and wife is by no means of such often occurrence as is generally believed in Europe; and it is almost unknown when both husband and wife are the property of the same master. Moreover, the general tendency of legislation in the Southern States is to prevent, as far as possible, the separation of husband and wife, without injury to the master, by depriving him of the right to rid himself of an unruly or insubordinate slave.

Prominent among the calumnies against the South which have unfortunately obtained credence in Europe, is the reproach of 'breeding slaves,' heaped upon the Southerners by their enemies, the Northern Abolitionists. We content ourselves here with stigmatizing this assertion as a malicious calumny; for not only is ' slave-breeding ' entirely unknown in the South, but no such thing has ever existed except in the fertile imaginations of the slanderers of the Southern people.

At the same time, the enemies of the South urge that without 'slave-breeding' there would be no material for the 'internal slave-trade' between the Southern States. But this is not true; for the internal slave-trade is limited partly to the sale of insubordinate slaves to other masters, as a penalty, which are thereby often rendered obedient and docile; and partly to emigration. In this case, where land has become too dear for the small proprietor in certain sections, he either disposes of his slaves to employ free labour, or emigrates to a new section, taking his slaves with him. Indeed, in many States there are laws prohibiting the introduction of slaves from other States, unless accompanied by their masters. The relative increase of the white and slave populations in certain States, and the corresponding slow increase of both in certain so-called 'slave-breeding States,' is a confirmation of this proposition.

On the other hand, what is the effect of slavery upon the slave-owner? It follows as a matter of course that, in so far as the master is not prohibited by the law, his relation to his slaves is such that he may be guilty of inhuman treatment. In another place we shall see how far the slave is protected against the arbitrary treatment of the master. Here it is sufficient to remark that, apart from all legal restraints, self-interest is as potent to prevent abuse of the slaves, as of any other kind of property, and that cruel treatment of slaves finds as little favour with public opinion as in the eyes of the law. No character would be less agreeable to a Southerner than the reputation of inhumanity towards his slaves. To suppose the contrary, were to assume that the Southern slave-holders are less civilized than others of their species in Europe. It is immaterial whether or not the master is in a position to abuse his slaves, if he should in passion impose no restraints upon his actions, when we reflect that in fact the case rarely, if ever, occurs; for in communities where slavery does not exist, similar cases constantly occur, as attested by the criminal returns. In both cases such unfortunate instances may be considered the result of accident. But, in truth, the slave-holder, who is accustomed to govern from his infancy, knows the necessity of moderation and kindness, in order to preserve subordination and respect among his slaves; and for this reason the slave-holder of the Southern States is, in an eminent degree, humane and forbearing.

The relation of the slave-holder guarantees him a purely independent position — allows him leisure for devoting his time to literature, science, and politics — affords opportunity for improvement of his tastes — enables him to reap the benefits of elevated social intercourse — and developes in him a more acute appreciation of what is noble, while producing a superior degree of refinement. The spirit of pure independence, which within proper limits can only be ennobling, is what essentially distinguishes the Southerner from the Northerner. The celebrated statesman, Burke, in speaking of the influence of slavery upon the Southern people in regard to their love of liberty, remarked —

' Where this is the case, those who are free are by far the most proud and jealous of their freedom. I cannot alter the nature of man. The fact is so; and these people of the Southern colonies are much more strongly, and with a higher and more stubborn spirit, attached to liberty than those to the North-ward. Such were all the ancient commonwealths, such were our Gothic ancestors, and such in our day were the Poles. Such will be all masters of slaves who are not slaves themselves. In such a people the haughtiness of domination combines itself with the spirit of freedom, fortifies it, and renders it invincible.'

When we reflect that the greatest statesmen of America—as Washington, Jefferson, Madison, Mon-roe, Calhoun, and others—were slave-holders, and that they were distinguished by their moderation and mildness, as well as ardent attachment to freedom, we may well entertain a doubt that the influence of slavery upon the dominant race in America has been pernicious; but the question arises, whether slavery is not rather a school for the developement of

SLAVERY NOT INJURIOUS TO THE WHITES.   147

virtue in the white race? But we have been told that 'there is no difficulty in tracing the injury inflicted by the system upon the master, upon the whole white population, or the sinister shadow which it casts over the face of society.' And, again, that 'there is an absolute injury sustained by the whole white community, apparent to any observer, and the more striking when contrasted with its condition in the neighbouring free States.' We beg for indulgence for our presumption, if we choose to challenge the truth of this sweeping charge. Is the 'injury of the system' visible in the refinement, intelligence, energy, courage, self-sacrifice, and perseverance of eight millions of Southerners, contending for their independence, under untold sufferings, against a remorseless, but more numerous enemy? Is it apparent in their regard for order, liberty, and the usages of civilization? Does this evince any degeneration? Or is 'the absolute injury sustained by the whole white community' observable in the proportionately greater number of colleges, schools, and churches in the South than in the North? Or is it rather to be 'observed' in the fact that the South has less than one-fifth as much crime and pauperism, in proportion to population, as the North? But, perhaps, as it is not visible in the moral or social condition of the Southern people, the 'injury of the system' may be found in its effects upon the agricultural products of the country. Let European industry, supplied by it, furnish the reply. It would seem as if 'no reasoning, no statistics, no profit, no philosophy,' could avail against the '*instincts*' of those who, while professing to know the condition of the Southern people, deliberately make such unfounded statements.

We hope that we may be borne with, if, in the examination of the objections to slavery, our reflections should lead us into some details, otherwise out of place. No end is heard of the assertion of the Northern Abolitionists, that one of the results of slavery is the unchastity of the female slaves, accompanied by a corresponding want of virtue on the part of the slaveholders. We do not deny that, in so far as the master abuses his power over his female slaves, to make them yield to vicious desires, he is responsible and reprehensible. But we do maintain that the notorious unchastity of the female slaves is not the consequence of slavery, but of their natural disposition for lust, which renders force superfluous. Every well-informed American knows, too, that cases of the application of force on the part of the master to seduce his slaves are unheard of, and that no instances are known of an abuse of power for such a purpose. The cause for this unchastity of the female slaves lies deeper: it is to be sought in their natural lewdness. Who does not know that the sacred obligations

of man and wife are not respected among the slaves
themselves? Still more is this true of their race in
Africa.   Indeed, we find a still lower moral condition
among the free negroes of the Northern States, where
marriage between the whites and blacks is either prohibited or unknown, than among the slaves, although
neither the scorching sun of the South is there to
develope the passion of lust, nor the 'lascivious slave-
holder' to accomplish his desires by violence.   According to the United States Census of 1850, of each
100 persons of the free coloured population, there
were in Maine 51, New Hampshire 54, Massachusetts 34, Connecticut 30, and Rhode Island 24,
mulattoes.   In Liberia and Sierra Leone the same
thing is notorious.*

As a political relation, the slavery of the Southern
States is a conservative element in the State.   First
of all, the effect of it is to equalize more nearly all
classes of the dominant race.   There are certain
kinds of menial labour which are never performed
by the whites, although not slave-holders.   Then,
too, the slave owes a certain respect and obedience
to every white person, poor or rich.   Consequently
every white man, be he a slave-owner or not, has
the consciousness that he belongs to the superior
race.   Hence it is that there is no conflict between
classes in the South.

* Bowen, 'Central Africa,' p. 32.

Moreover, there is no conflict between capital and labour, for the labourer is himself capital. Among the systems of labour in use in Europe this conflict is perpetually going on. Brilliant theories have been devised to remove the ever-present enmity between these two great forces of human progress; but all have been of no avail. The difficulty has as yet been obviated only by slavery.

Again, little attraction is offered for emigration to the Southern States, for only capitalists, who may acquire property in slaves, find it to their interests to emigrate thither. By this means the South has been protected from the outpourings of the dregs of European society.

It has been remarked that the situation of the slave-owner qualifies him, in an eminent degree, for discharging the duties of a free citizen. His leisure enables him to cultivate his intellectual powers, and his condition of independence places him beyond the reach of demagogues and corruption. In this way he is preeminently suited for filling the highest political stations in the Government. Therefore, such positions are not coveted for the income they yield, but only out of a patriotic ambition. When the slave-owner occupies an official position, he receives the acknowledgement of his fellow-citizens, who have all the same interests and the same opinions as himself. Consequently he does not fear to be subverted by the intrigues of demagogues; and political humbug is unknown.

Slavery is, also, a great protection against pauperism; for the labouring class, being slaves, must by law be supported by their owners.*

Need it be said that it is not in consequence of slave labour, as asserted by Northern Abolitionists, that the soil of the South is soon exhausted? The kind of crops produced, known as 'clean crops,' cause the soil in the South soon to become impoverished, unless much attention is paid to enriching it. For the naked-ploughed soil is exposed to the scorching southern sun for a considerable part of the year, which, as every agriculturist is aware, has a most deleterious effect upon it. This would hold equally true, whether free or slave labour were employed.

The generally accepted law that free labour is cheaper than slave labour, finds no application in the South. There is no doubt that where the labouring population is very dense, as in certain parts of Europe, where the free man must work or starve, free labour is cheaper than any other; for no capital is then needed to be employed in owning labour. In this case free labour must and will drive out involuntary labour. But the question assumes quite a different

* An interesting example is afforded by the Abstract of the Seventh Census, p. 28, according to which, in 1850, Rhode Island, with 147,545 inhabitants, had 2,560 paupers, while Georgia, with a population of 524,503 free whites, had only 1,036 paupers.

phase when we attempt to apply the principle to labour in the South. In the first place, there is no such abundance of free labour to be had there; while the climate makes it almost throughout impossible for the white man to work. He cannot support the damp hot atmosphere and the miasma of the Savannas. Were it, however, possible to acclimatize the whites in that region, and were a thick white population to be obtained, such free labour would not be adapted to the cultivation of the Southern products, such as rice, sugar, tobacco, and cotton. A species of labour is needed for these productions, which is not liable to be disturbed by 'strikes' or accident. It is indispensable to have a system of organized, regular, and uninterrupted labour, in order to make the production of rice, sugar, tobacco, and cotton profitable. If the negro slaves were free, we know full well from experience that they would not work without compulsion. As long, therefore, as the climate of the South remains an insuperable obstacle in the way of the white man, and as long as no means can be devised for counteracting the natural indolence and want of self-respect of the negro, which prefer theft to industry, involuntary or slave labour must remain the only possible labour for the South, and, therefore, the cheapest that can be employed for its products. The labour of the South is chiefly of a nature which requires physical strength, endurance, and uniformity, without the capacity for judgement, as in skilled labour. For such labour the African slave is alone adapted.

II. *Status of the Slaves.*

With the Romans, the slave was considered as a *chattel* (*res*). As such the Roman slave was deprived of the right of personal liberty, and the right of property. The power of life and death, 'jus vitæ necisque,' also belonged to the master.

The status of the slave in the Southern States is, on the contrary, a double one. On the one hand, the slave is a chattel; but, on the other, a legal protection has been accorded to him, through the instrumentality of Christianity and the developement of human civilization, by which his condition has been ameliorated materially. The slave is, therefore, by reason of his thus modified condition, also a *person*, and his *legal person* is by no means so subordinate as is generally supposed in Europe. Prominent is the protection accorded to life and to limb.

Throughout all the States where slavery exists, the homicide of a slave is made by law to be murder. In the case of the killing of a slave by his master, or any other person, the slayer incurs the same penalty as if the slave had been a free white. Consequently,

it appears that there is no difference at all in the
legal protection accorded to the life of a slave and of
a free citizen. The presumption of malice, also, holds
in the case of the homicide of a slave, and the rule
with regard to the burden of the proof is identically
the same as in the homicide of free white persons.
It will be evident that this rule of the law must react
with great severity upon the slayer, in cases where
there are no competent witnesses to the deed, as may
most likely occur from the private relation of the
master to his slave, separated from the public view
on his plantation. Although this legal protection
of life and personal security is accorded to the slave,
and becomes thereby a quasi right, his natural condition, as owing obedience and subordination, does
not justify him in repelling force by force to the
same extent, as in the case of a freeman. Still the
law in its mercy does justify the slave in using
force to repel force when his life or limb is endan-
gered, even if in defence he slays the aggressor.[*]
To this extent, then, the rule of the civil law—'vim
vi defendere, omnes leges omniaque jura permittunt'
—is applicable to slaves.

The slave enjoys the protection of the law not only
with reference to life, but also against violent and

---

[*] The State v. Will, a negro, 1 Dev. and Bat. 121–165 —a celebrated
case, decided by Judge Gaston ; the case decided by Judge Thatcher ;
and others cited by Cobb, vol. i. p. 94.

cruel treatment. The decision of what constitutes
cruelty must, in many instances, be left to the decision of the jury.   'The general principle would be,
that the master's right to enforce obedience and subordination on the part of the slave, should, as far as
possible, remain intact. Whatever goes beyond this,
and from mere wantonness or revenge inflicts pain and
suffering, especially unusual and inhuman punishments, is cruelty, and should be punished as such.
And though the statute creating the offence specifies
particular acts of cruelty, yet it has been held, that
other acts of cruelty, though of a minor grade than
those specified, were indictable under the general
description of cruel punishments.'*

It is also held that, where a slave is unduly excited
by the cruel treatment of his master, this circumstance is sufficient to extenuate the offence committed under the provocation; and if a homicide
be committed under these circumstances, the provocation serves as a rebuttal of the presumption of
malice.†

Legal counsel is afforded the slave in all cases
where he is accused. The laws of many States
make it the duty of the Court, ipso jure, to appoint
counsel for the accused slave; in many others the
master is required to provide counsel, where he is

---

* Cobb, p. 98 ; and the cases there cited.
† Ibidem.

not a party; and, this failing, it is made incumbent on the Court. Here the slave is regarded as a ward of the Court.

Having found that the slave is protected as to his life and personal security, it remains to be seen how far the third great right of a free citizen under the Common Law — the right of personal liberty — is affected by the condition of slavery. Herein is visible the great inferiority of the slave to the freeman. This is what constitutes him a slave; he has no liberty but that allowed him by his master. Without this quality he would, in fact, cease to be a slave. But while admitting this fact, it must not be forgotten that the slave does enjoy a certain amount of liberty in the leisure granted to him during the Sabbath, the holidays, and the night. When his day's labour is over, the negro slave is free to enjoy himself in any legitimate way he may choose, there being no cares for the morrow to impair his pleasures. In fact, the slave does in this way enjoy as much, or more, real liberty than the free white labourer of the same class in Europe. It is hardly necessary to observe that the master has a legal right to capture his fugitive slave at any time, and wherever he may find him. This right is not subject to the prescription of time.

As to the nature of the punishments inflicted upon slaves convicted of offences, it may be remarked that, as the slave, from his nature, cannot be reached by the ordinary penalties of fine and imprisonment, having neither property nor liberty of which he may be deprived, his body offers the only means of inflicting punishment. Consequently all offences are made to fall under two categories, — capital offences and offences punishable by whipping.* The opera-tion of this principle is to make the punishment for many offences much lighter, while, on the other hand, some offences are punished with more rigour than in the case of free citizens. The policy of the law makes this often necessary, and it is exemplified in the fact that rape of a white female, arson in towns, attempts to poison, and insurrection, are made capital crimes. Investigation will show, however, that the relation of the master to his slaves, by giving him a certain police authority over them, is most beneficent to the negro race. Crime is prevented more effectually, and the rigours of the law are made to press less heavily upon the slave, than in the case of free negroes, while the general benefit accruing to society is incalculable.

With regard to the jurisdiction of the Courts over crime, it is provided by law that the highest Circuit Courts are alone competent to take cognizance of the acts of slaves accused of capital crimes; while the

---

* The exceptions to this rule are Virginia and Maryland, which have laws inflicting transportation for certain offences committed by slaves.

accused must have a fair trial by a jury; in which
case the procedure is identical as in the trial of free
citizens, with the single exception that negroes—free
and slave—are competent witnesses for or against
slaves. The good character of an accused slave
may also be offered in evidence, and works a rebuttal
of the presumption of guilt; but his bad character
cannot be taken into consideration, except in the
same cases as with free white. Less value must also
be attached to the confessions of a slave tending to
incriminate himself, because of his habits of obedience.

Although the master is entitled to claim obedience
and subordination from his slave, he dare not kill or
maim him to enforce them. But in all the States
the infliction of moderate corporal punishment is
placed in the power and discretion of the master.

Insubordination, insurrection, and rebellion, are
crimes which are punished by the State.

As a consequence of the inferior position of the
slave as a person, there are, necessarily, many disabilities attaching to his condition. One of the principal of these is the incapacity to be a witness. This
is not, however, absolute, as the slave is capable of
giving evidence, both for and against other slaves
and free negroes. Still, under no circumstances can
a slave be a witness for or against a white person
in any Southern States; and this right on principle.
It is not difficult to understand that the time-

honoured maxim, requiring a witness to be a freeman, 'liber et legalis homo,' acquires increased force
when it is a question of conferring the privilege of
testifying upon a race, held in subjection, accustomed
to obedience, and notorious for its mendacity. That
making the negro '*othesworth*' would be most unfortunate for the race, as well as for the masters, is
conceded by even the most uncompromising enemies
of slavery,* on account of 'the general presumption
against his moral character, more especially in the
article of veracity.' † The same rule incapacitating
slaves for testifying where free whites are concerned,
is not limited to the Southern States, but holds in
every State of the old American Union.‡ Again,
in several of the Northern States this abridgement
of the credibility of slaves as witnesses has been
extended to both free-born and emancipated negroes.
So we find that in Indiana, Illinois, Iowa, and Ohio,
no person of the negro race can be a witness for or
against whites, but only in the case where slaves or
free negroes are parties.

The slave cannot, by law, acquire property: all
that he gains becomes the property of his master.
The rule with respect to villains in England formerly,
'quicquid acquiritur servo acquiritur domino,'§ as

* Stephen, on West Ind. Slavery, vol. i. p. 177.
† Ibidem.
‡ See Case of Winn. Adm., &c., versus Jones, 6 Leigh, 74.
§ Co. Litt. Lib. ii. § 172.

announced by my Lord Coke, holds with regard to
the slaves in the Southern States. Nevertheless, a
'peculium ex gratia domini' is allowed in all the States,
and, exceptionally, by statute in Louisiana. And no
master would ever think of depriving his slave of
any property gained by labour in his leisure hours,
or acquired by accident or gift. To do this would
be sufficient to exclude such a master from good
society wherever it should be known. In many
ways the slaves do acquire considerable means for
extra comfort, as it is the custom to permit them
to cultivate a part of the soil for their own benefit during their leisure hours. The products of
such labour are sold with the crops of the master, or
paid for by him, and the proceeds given to the slaves
for their individual use. Custom, in this way, allows
the slave the actual enjoyment of that which he
cannot claim by law.

Furthermore, the slave is incapacitated to contract; and contracts when made with slaves cannot
be enforced. The Roman slave also laboured under
the same disability; but there was this slight difference—that contracts made by the Roman slave
could be enforced to the extent of his peculium, and
after manumission he could demand the fulfilment
of engagements entered into during his former
servitude.

A consequence of the disability of slaves to contract

is their inability to contract marriage at law. But still there exists a state of matrimony, which is solemnized by the church, and considered as binding between the parties. It is a kind of contubernium, which is mercifully recognised by the law in cases of offences between parents and children, so far as it is a question of the motive. It results from this contubernial relation that the laws of several States absolutely forbid the separation of slave-parents and children;—and the general tendency of legislation in the South is to prevent, as far as possible, the separation of families.

The slave may act as the agent of his master with his authorization, in which case the master is responsible for his acts. In only a few cases do exceptions to this rule occur, where it would be impolitic to place the slaves in a position to inflict injury upon others.

It follows, also, from the incapacity of a slave to contract and acquire property, that he cannot be a party to a suit in a Court of Law. There is one exception only—the suit for freedom, actio de liberali caussa—which may be brought by a slave, who is free, but unlawfully deprived of his freedom. This action is purely personal, and cannot, therefore, be instituted by anyone else than the slave interested; it is not subject to the 'limitation of actions;' and even in case that the slave entitled to freedom allows

M

himself to be sold without making mention of the fact, this cannot bar his right to bring the action at any future time.

We have attempted above to give a brief idea of the protection thrown around the slave by the law, as well as of his disabilities. No effort has been made to depict the condition of the slave in the Southern States as better than it is; and while admitting the duty of the Southern people to direct legislation so as to avoid, the most possible, any abuses that might arise from accidental circumstances, we maintain that the condition of the slave is at present far from being oppressive, and that servitude in the South is free from the greater evils attaching to other systems of slavery with which we are acquainted.

III. *Manumission and Emancipation.*

The manumission of slaves in America is almost coeval with the introduction of slavery upon that continent. Individual cases of it have always been allowed, and there have never been wanting persons to bestow the gift of liberty on their slaves. Too frequently has the right to manumit been abused in America; and this has resulted in the enactment of laws in certain States, by which restraints are

placed upon it. Obviously it is contrary to the
public policy to permit a numerous class of indolent
and vicious persons to be cast as a burden upon the
State. To prevent such a deplorable result, restrictions have, very properly, in some States been
imposed upon the right of manumission. Among
these is the enactment, that liberated slaves be
required to quit the State. It has also very wisely
been forbidden to free the aged, young, decrepit,
and sick, who would be unable to provide for themselves, and thus become a burden and expense to
the Commonwealth; and the obligation to care for
such slaves is made incumbent upon the master.
Consequently, in some instances, a certain age is
fixed by law, before and after which manumission
shall not be permitted. On the other hand, the
master has not the right, under any circumstances,
to free his slaves with intent to defraud his cre-
ditors. With the exception of these restrictions,
there is no impediment to manumission of the slaves
in the Southern States.

The forms to be observed in liberating slaves
are not unnecessarily strict. Manumission may be
.effected in presenti, in futuro, by parol, by writing,
and by inference. In some States, however, it is
not allowed to free slaves by testament directly,
as in Alabama, Maryland, and Mississippi; but even
here it may be accomplished indirectly when the

testator imposes it upon his executor testamenti in his will.

It must not, however, be supposed that the slave, in becoming free, thereby acquires the rights of a citizen. With the exception of a few Northern States, the free negro nowhere enjoys the privilege of citizenship; and, as was decided in the Dred Scott case,* the negro cannot become a citizen of the United States. In the Southern States the condition of the free negroes is not very different from that of the dedititii among the citizens of Rome; they are under the supervision of the police, are not allowed to bear arms, and, from considerations of public policy, are not permitted to hold property in slaves. The free negro must also have a *prochein ami* or patronus in the South, who contracts for him.

The amalgamation of whites with blacks operates to disqualify the issue for the rights of free citizens in the entire South and in many Northern States.

One of the most interesting and instructive fields for investigation is furnished by the examination of the influence of liberty upon the race of African negroes. Experiments have been made in the Northern States, where slavery was abolished years ago, in the West Indies and in Africa. The results in the Northern States, as stated by Northern men, and confirmed by the census returns, are furnished by Cobb in his

---

* Scott versus Sanford, 19. Howard, S. C. 1.

excellent work, to which reference has already been
made.   We extract the following :*—

'The number of negroes emancipated in the United
States were comparatively small, but the effects do
not vary materially, as to their condition, from those
already noticed.   The fact of their limited number,
as well as the additional facts, that previous to their
emancipation they were employed but little in agricultural pursuits, and that the nature of the agriculture of the Northern States of the Union was illy
suited to this species of labour, protected the prosperity of those States from the depressing influences
experienced elsewhere from the abolition of slavery.
That their physical condition does not compare
favourably with that of the slaves of the South, is
evident from the decennial census of the United
States, showing a much larger increase in the latter
than in the former.   No surer test can be applied.

'In order to obtain accurate information, I sent a
circular to the Governors and leading politicians of
the non-slaveholding States.   I received answers as
follows : —

'*Maine*, Hon. I. J. D. Fuller.

'*Vermont*, Hon. J. Meacham.

'*Connecticut*, Gov. Pond, and Hon. O. S. Seymour.

'*Rhode Island*, Hon. B. B. Thurston.

'*New Jersey*, Gov. Foot.

* Cobb. ch. xv. p. cci. *et seq.*

'*New York*, Hon. S. G. Haven.
'*Pennsylvania*, Hon. E. D. Ingraham.
'*Indiana*, Gov. Wright.
'*Illinois*, Gov. Matteson, Hon. W. A. Richardson.
'*Iowa*, Judge Mason, Hon. Mr. Hern.
'*Michigan*, Gov. Parsons.'

A. *With Reference to the Physical Condition.*

Maine. — 'The condition of the negro population varies; but is very far below the whites.'

Vermont. — 'Their condition and character have great varieties. They are not in as good a condition as the whites.'

Connecticut. — Gov. Pond says: 'The condition of the negro population, as a class, is not thrifty, and does not compare favourably with the whites. There are many, comparatively speaking, who are industrious.'

Rhode Island. — 'They are, generally, industrious and frugal.'

New Jersey. — 'Their condition is debased; with few exceptions very poor; generally indolent.'

New York. — 'The condition of the negro is diversified, — some prosperous, some industrious. They have no social relations with the whites. Generally on about the same level that whites would occupy with like antecedent.'

Pennsylvania. — 'I deem the condition of the negro population in this State to be that of a degraded class, much deteriorated by freedom. They are not industrious.'

Indiana. — 'They are not prosperous. The majority of them are not doing well. We have sent off thirty or forty this year to Liberia, and hope to send off one hundred or more, next year, and finally to get rid of all we have in the State, and do not intend to have another negro or mulatto come into the State.'

Illinois. — 'As a class, they are thriftless and idle. Their condition far inferior to that of the whites.' (Gov.) 'About the towns and cities, idle and dissolute, with exceptions. In the rural districts, many are industrious and prosperous.' (H. Richardson.)

Iowa. — 'Very few negroes in Iowa. Far above the condition of those met with in our Eastern cities.'

Michigan. — 'Tolerably prosperous. Far behind the white population.'

B. *With Reference to the Intellectual Condition.*

Maine. — 'Admitted into the public schools with the whites. Very far below them in education.'

Vermont. — 'Generally able to read and write; a few are liberally educated; not like the whites.'

Connecticut. — 'Fall much below the whites in education.'

Rhode Island.—'Some are educated in the district schools. Compare well with the whites of their condition.'

New Jersey.—'Generally ignorant. Far below the whites in intelligence.'

New York.—'Generally very poorly, or but little educated.'

Pennsylvania.—'Not educated. It is remarkable that almost all the decent and respectable negroes we have, have been household slaves in some Southern State.'

Indiana.—'Not educated.'

Illinois.—'Ignorant.' (Gov.)

Michigan.—'Not generally educated. Far below the whites.'

C. *With Reference to the Moral Condition.*

Maine.—'Far below the whites.'

Vermont.—'Not as good as the whites.'

Connecticut.—'Does not compare favourably with the whites.' (Gov.) 'They are, with us, an inferior caste; and in morality fall much below the whites.' (Seymour.)

New Jersey.—'Immoral; vicious animal propensities; drunkenness, theft, and promiscuous sexual intercourse quite common. One-fourth of the criminals in the State prison are coloured persons; while they constitute only one twenty-fifth of the population.'

New York.—'Diversified; some moral.'

Pennsylvania.—'Immoral. I am satisfied, from forty years' attention to the subject, that the removal of the wholesome restraint of slavery, and the consequent absence of the stimulus of the coercion to labour of that condition, have materially affected their condition for the worse. They exhibit all the characteristics of an inferior race, to whose personal comfort, happiness, and morality, the supervision, restraint, and coercion of a superior race seem absolutely necessary.'

Indiana.—'In many instances very immoral.'

Illinois.—'Thriftless, idle, ignorant, and vicious.' (Gov.) 'In towns and cities dissolute, with exceptions.' (Richardson.)

Iowa.—'Of a fair character.'

Michigan.—'Tolerably moral. Far below the whites.'

'Notwithstanding the very laboured efforts made for their intellectual improvement, taken as a body, they have made no advancement. Averse to physical labour, they are equally averse to intellectual effort. The young negro acquires readily the first rudiments of education, where memory and imitation are chiefly brought into action, but for any higher effort of reason and judgement he is, as a general rule, utterly incapable.

'His moral condition compares unfavorably with

that of the slave of the South.   He seeks the cities
and towns, and indulges freely in those vices to
which his nature inclines him.   His friends inveigh
against " the prejudice of colour," but he rises no
higher in Mexico, Central America, New Grenada,
or Brazil, where no such prejudice exists.   The
cause lies deeper: in the nature and constitution of
the negro race.

'The emancipated negroes do not enjoy full and
equal civil and political rights in any State in the
Union, except the State of Vermont.   In several of
the States they are not permitted to vote,* in some
under peculiar restrictions.†   In almost every State
where the matter has been made a subject of legislation, inter-marriages with the whites are forbidden.‡   In none are such marriages at all common.§   In many they are forbidden to serve as jurors,
or to be sworn as witnesses against a white person,‖
or hold any elective office.¶

'The criminal statistics of the slaveholding and
non-slaveholding States show that the proportion of

* Connecticut, New Jersey, Pennsylvania, Indiana, Illinois, Iowa,
Michigan.

† New York.

‡ Maine, Rhode Island, Indiana, Illinois, Michigan.

§ Connecticut.—Issue cannot vote. New Jersey.—No legislation, and
no cases of such marriage. New York.—Issue considered as blacks.
Pennsylvania.—Issue considered as blacks.   Iowa.—No such cases.

‖ Connecticut, New Jersey, Indiana, Illinois, Iowa.

¶ Connecticut, New Jersey, Pennsylvania, Indiana, Illinois, Michigan.

crime committed by negroes in the former does not
reach the ratio of this population as compared with
the whites,* while in the latter the ratio is much
greater.   The same is true of the statistics of mortality and disease.   The apparent disproportion in
the former case is greater than the truth, as many
petty crimes by slaves do not reach the courts;
and in the latter, it may be truly said that the
Southern climate is more favourable to the health
and longevity of the negro.   But making due allow-
ances in both cases for these causes, it is still true,
that the negroes are less addicted to crime, and more
healthy and long-lived, in a state of slavery than of
freedom.'†

In spite of the skill of the British philanthropists,
all efforts to save the free negroes in the West Indies
have proved vain; Jamaica and the other English
islands are retrograding at a pace that astonishes
even the enemies of slavery.   Hayti affords a picture
of barbarism already attained; while little more can
be said in favour of Mexico.   Liberia and Sierra

* Judge Starnes, of Georgia, published several articles, giving statistics
on this point, worthy of a more lasting existence than derived from the
columns of a newspaper.

† In giving my conclusions as to the free negroes of the North, I have
relied on numberless authorities, combined with personal observation.   I
subjoin only a few : Paulding, on Slavery ; 'Abolition, a Sedition,' by
a Northern Man ; Bishop Hopkins's ' American Citizen,' p. 135 ; ' Seaboard Slave States,' p. 125 ; ' Reports of American Colonization Society ;'
' Report of Naval Committee of House of Representatives on Establishing
a Line of Mail Steamers to Liberia' (1850) ; 'Negromania,' by John
Campbell : being a Collection of Papers by distinguished men.

Leone corroborate the conclusions at which we have arrived in regard to the African negroes in the New World. And the history of the race in Africa confirms the experience of modern times. This has been expressed most briefly by a distinguished French authority as follows:—'Ni les sciences de l'Egypte, ni la puissance commerciale de Carthage, ni la domination des Romains en Afrique, n'ont pu faire pénétrer chez eux la civilisation.'*

On the other hand, it seems well established that the negro approaches more nearly a state of civilization, experiences the greatest happiness, and attains the highest degree of developement of which his nature is susceptible, in a state of bondage. And, though the race may be thus elevated to a semi-civilization while in a state of slavery, as soon as it is emancipated, it commences instantly to relapse in that hopeless barbarism from which the superior race had raised it. Charles Hamilton Smith, an Englishman, says of them, 'They have never comprehended what they have learned, nor retained a civilization taught them by contact with more refined nations, as soon as that contact had ceased.'† Again, Carlyle, in addressing himself to the emancipated slaves of the West Indies, gives an excellent common-sense view

* Levavasseur, 'Esclavage de la Race Noire,' p. 77.

† Charles H. Smith, 'Natural History of Human Species: its Typical Forms,' &c., p. 196.

of the question. He says, ' You are not slaves now! Nor do I wish, if it can be avoided, to see you slaves again; but decidedly, you will have to be servants to those that are born wiser than you, that are born lords of you; servants to the whites if they are (as what mortal man can doubt they are?) born wiser than you. That you may depend on it, my obscure black friends, is and was always the law of the world for you and for all men to be servants, the more foolish of us to the more wise. . . . . Heaven's laws are not repealable by earth, however earth may try.'* With history and experience to enlighten us, no room seems left to doubt the baneful influence of liberty upon the negroes, whether it be in their own Africa, or in the midst of the white race.

From the moment of the breaking out of the war, the question of the emancipation of the slaves in the Southern States has not ceased to be agitated. For the Southerners, and for Europeans too, this question has a practical side. First of all, the enquiry presents itself, Is a general emancipation possible? No reasonable person will contend that under any circumstances emancipation could be advocated, without indemnification for the parties interested. The first insurmountable obstacle, then, to be encountered is the amount of property represented by the slaves. The number of these is about 4,000,000; and if we

* Letter on Rights of Negroes.

calculate their average value at 125l. per head, a low
estimate before the commencement of the war, we
shall find their total worth to be 500,000,000l. Now
Mr. Lincoln has proposed to Congress to pass a law
for the indemnification of slave-holders in those
States that might be disposed to abolish slavery.
But if it could be supposed that the Southern States,
intimidated by Lincoln's proclamation of emancipation, should suddenly become 'loyal' to the Union,
and then determine to abolish slavery, how would it
be possible for Congress to obtain any considerable
part of the sum of 500,000,000l., in view of the fact
that the Federal Government is already almost a
declared bankrupt? Can the idea be entertained for
a moment that the Northern people would impose a
tax upon themselves, necessary to raise this amount,
out of love for the negroes? The manner in which
the free negro is treated in the North will furnish
the best reply.

Should slave labour be abolished in the South,
the landed property that would thereby become
valueless or unprofitable may be estimated at quite
half of the value of the slaves. Thus we should have
for the entire *immediate* interests, which would be
ruined by emancipation, the respectable amount of
750,000,000l.— a sum just 37½ times as large as that
paid by England for emancipating her slaves in the
West Indies.

Another point for consideration is the probable effect of emancipation upon the industry, commerce, and prosperity of the world. The influence of slave labour for the advancement of the civilization and prosperity of the world has been incalculable. The universal suffering that has already resulted from the interruption of the supply of the products of slave labour, during the present war, may serve as a slight indication of that general misery which would be felt throughout the civilized world, and nowhere more than in England, should these products be cut off permanently, by the destruction of the organized system of labour in the Southern States.

The third and not least important point to be examined is the condition of the 4,000,000 of slaves, after emancipation. Amalgamation is out of the question; for not only does the ineradicable antipathy of the white race in America for the negro place this result beyond the possibility of accomplishment, but, if practicable, it would be only a scheme for degrading our nature to the lowest point of barbarism. Rejecting this idea of a mixture of the races, we should find that emancipation would not obtain social or political equality for the negroes. Never will the Southern people consent to accord these to a race so far beneath themselves in the scale of human developement. Thus there would be a class in the State, neither citizens nor slaves, which would not labour without compulsion, and soon would commence a conflict of races and of classes, that would terminate only in the extermination of one or the other. Can any one doubt which side would be victorious? Are the philanthropists willing and prepared to accomplish the liberation of the negro slaves at the price of the annihilation of their race in America? Is, indeed, the *benefit* worthy of the *sacrifice*? Can any reasonable man, then, hesitate to oppose general emancipation, as being impracticable and unwise? From the foregoing considerations we think ourselves justified in asserting that a general emancipation of the 4,000,000 of slaves in the Southern States is not only impossible, but would be the greatest misfortune for the slaves themselves, and an incalculable evil for mankind in general.

Should, however, slave labour in the South cease to be the most profitable, or should the products of the South become unnecessary to the civilized world, or should the slaves be changed, either by a miracle or by the influence of slavery, so as to become capable of enjoying liberty, slavery will disappear of itself. All history teaches us that no people have ever been retained permanently in bondage, if they were fit for freedom. Until, therefore, these results shall be accomplished, slavery will remain a benefit to the slaves, a necessity for the human race, and the inheritance of the Southerners. If slavery is ever to be abolished in the South, the future will provide the means at the proper time.

In conclusion, it is to be regretted that the impression has been produced in Europe, that the Confederate States would be willing to enter into an engagement with the powers of Europe in relation to slavery, as the price of recognition. For what are the people of the Confederate States making such sacrifices, and submitting to such sufferings at present? What is the object of the war, if not to vindicate the right to govern themselves as they think proper? They may not 'desire a state of permanent conflict with the opinions of all the great civilized powers,' but it is simply absurd to suppose that they would carry on such a war, in order to make a surrender of their independence, as soon as achieved, by submitting to any dictation whatever from foreign powers in relation to their municipal regulations.

LONDON

PRINTED BY SPOTTISWOODE AND CO

NEW-STREET SQUARE

www.ingramcontent.com/pod-product-compliance
Lightning Source LLC
Chambersburg PA
CBHW030321270326
41926CB00010B/1458